THE
EXCEPTIONAL
SEVEN PERCENT

THE
EXCEPTIONAL
SEVEN PERCENT

The Nine Secrets of the World's Happiest Couples

Gregory K. Popcak, MSW

CITADEL PRESS
Kensington Publishing Corp.
www.kensingtonbooks.com

CITADEL PRESS books are published by

Kensington Publishing Corp.
850 Third Avenue
New York, NY 10022

All Kensington titles, imprints, and distributed lines are available at special quantity discounts for bulk purchases for sales promotions, premiums, fund raising, educational, or institutional use. Special book excerpts or customized printings can also be created to fit specific needs. For details, write or phone the office of the Kensington special sales manager: Kensington Publishing Corp., 850 Third Avenue, New York, NY 10022, attn: Special Sales Department, phone 1-800-221-2647.

Kensington and the K logo Reg. U.S. Pat. & TM Office
Citadel Press is a trademark of Kensington Publishing Corp.

First printing 2000

10 9 8 7 6 5 4 3 2 1

Printed in the United States of America

Library of Congress Cataloging-in-Publication Data

Popcak, Gregory K.
    The exceptional seven percent : nine secrets of the world's
happiest couples / by Gregory K. Popcak.
        p.   cm.
    Includes index.
    ISBN 1-55972-505-2
    1. Marriage.   2. Married people—Psychology.   3. Married people—
Conduct of life.   I. Title.
HQ734.P753   1999
306.85—dc21   99-14066
                                                        CIP

Contents

Preface

*The sum which two married people owe to one
another defies calculation. It is an infinite debt, which
can only be discharged throughout all eternity.*

—GOETHE

I AM PLEASED to be able to say that my wife and I have always had a
better than average *relationship*. But about three years into our
marriage, we both came to a point where we wanted more. We
wanted to grow more as persons and deepen the intimacy we
experienced in our daily lives together. When we would mention this
in passing to other couples they would just laugh at us. Weren't we
being unrealistic? We already had a *good* marriage. What more could
we possibly want?

As I understand the problem now, I see that even though my wife
and I were doing many of the things the marriage gurus of the time
said must be done in order to have a good marriage, having a *great*
relationship takes more than an armload of techniques. It requires a
husband and wife striving to become the most complete people they
can be in their own right, and it requires the couple to acknowledge
the actualizing power of their marriage.

The word "actualization" may be unfamiliar to some readers.
Basically, it refers to every human being's drive to become the most
fulfilled and competent person possible. According to psychologist
Abraham Maslow, who studied "self-actualizing people," these individuals exhibit such qualities as acceptance of themselves and others,

spontaneity, creativity, compassion, inner peace, a healthy sense of humor, and the capacity for extraordinarily deep intimacy. Likewise, self-actualizers are often considered to be living, breathing examples of their own unique value system. In short, they are the people we all want to be when we "grow up."

What, you might ask, made my wife and I think that marriage had such a thing as actualizing potential? Moreover, what made us think we could use our *relationship* to help us become such people? It is a commonly held belief among couples therapists that marriage has powerful transformative properties. Psychotherapist and author Harville Hendrix has asserted that marriage has an awesome potential to heal old emotional scars, and this sentiment is echoed by the preeminent family therapist, author, and lecturer Cloé Madanes, who has said that "marriage is the most powerful form of group therapy we know." My wife and I reasoned that if marriage had the power to heal emotional scars, wasn't it possible that marriage also had the power to raise two basically healthy people to a greater level of competence, consciousness, spiritual awareness, and psychological fulfillment?

Sadly, these questions coincided with the conception and subsequent miscarriage of our first child. The sorrow we felt after this experience led to a great deal of soul searching. My wife and I needed to draw support from each other in ways we never anticipated and that few could guide us through. If we were going to make it through this difficult time, we had to apply, in earnest, all the things we were learning to help each other and our marriage grow stronger in light of what was, for us, a terrible tragedy.

In the years since that loss, my wife and I have come to see that our first child—short though his life was—gave us a great gift. Ultimately, it was the gift of his life and death that forced us to lay aside conventional expectations of marriage and family life and demand more of ourselves and each other. Looking back, though we have weathered many storms since, were it not for that particular experience, my wife and I would not be the partners and parents we are today. To honor this fact, we named the child who gave his life for our transformation Isaiah, after the Old Testament prophet who Christians believe spoke of the great blessings the future held for those who persisted faithfully through trial.

In my journey as both a husband and a psychotherapist, I have found that having an exceptional marriage requires challenging one's selfishness on a daily basis. This is the source of unending struggle for me, because at my core I am a pretty selfish person. And so, like a recovering alcoholic who maintains his sobriety by refusing to take the first drink, I attempt to abstain from selfishness by consciously avoiding opportunities to be lazy in my love. I am certainly no better than anyone else, in fact I am probably worse, but perhaps I try harder because every day in my office I see how easy it is to fall off the wagon (as it were) and what the consequences are. On those days when I feel I am too tired or too irritated to love, I force myself to think of the person I would become if I *didn't* make the choice to love. And then I imagine the person I *could become* simply by getting off the sofa and serving my wife or my children, by being the first person to say "I'm sorry," by seeking out ways to show my family how valuable they are to me, by looking for things to do around the house that will make their lives easier or more pleasant. When I put those two images side by side, it is not difficult to choose which path to take, even though my emotions are sometimes loathe to admit it.

But it is not all work. My wife and I have reaped many rewards for our efforts in the form of greater competency as human beings and deeper intimacy as a couple. And we are still traveling. More than anything else, this book is an invitation to join us in the walk down a road that never ends, but leads to new joys, challenges, and celebrations around every bend.

The Exceptional Seven Percent is about the rules, attitudes, and behaviors practiced in exceptional marriages, all of which have been suggested by research, validated by my own professional and personal observations, and, ultimately, tested in my own marriage with fabulous results. Each chapter of this book will examine one of the nine basic traits of exceptional couples in detail. More important each chapter will explain the steps you must take to enable those traits to flourish in your own marriage.

The stories and case examples you will read are true. I have, however, significantly changed identifying details for the sake of confidentiality. Likewise, when a couple's story *in vivo* evolved over the period of several weeks or months, I have taken the liberty of reporting the story in the fictional first person, for the sake of brevity. Please be assured, however, that although the stories have been dramatized, I have taken great pains to make certain the language accurately represents the actual ideas and events the original couples shared with me.

A second technical note. This book is addressed to both the husband and the wife. However, it has not always been possible to use both personal pronouns (for example, "he" and "she") throughout the text. Though I may in a given context say that, "he must do X" or, "she must do Y," I am in every case speaking to and about *both* partners.

It is my hope that as you read these pages you will discover the secrets to building the marriage you have always wanted but never dreamed was possible.

Let the good lovin' begin!

Acknowledgments

WHILE IT has been my privilege to put these words to paper, I would not have been able to credibly write a single sentence if this book had not already been "written" in the daily life of my marriage. In this all-important sense, I wish to credit my wife as a true coauthor. She has allowed our marriage to be the laboratory for everything in *The Exceptional Seven Percent*. In addition to being a truly good woman, an enviable mother, and a generous lover, she is my best critic, my most astute advisor, and a patient editor. To me, she is everything God created woman to be, and I am daily blessed by her loving presence.

Likewise, I offer my gratitude to the people at Carol Publishing Group, specifically Carrie Cantor, for generously supporting this project; my agent, Jennifer Blose, at the Lee Shore Literary Agency; and B.V.M. (you know who you are) for her gentle guidance throughout the years.

THE
EXCEPTIONAL
SEVEN PERCENT

1

Who Are the Exceptional Seven Percent?

There is no more lovely, friendly, and charming
relationship, communion or company than a good
marriage.

—MARTIN LUTHER

I CALL IT THE *I-dare-you-to-make-me-love-my-mate* stare.

That was the look Jack and Alicia had on their faces as they sat across from me in my marriage counseling office. It's a look I'm accustomed to, and frankly, I have come to enjoy the challenge it presents for me, because I know a secret. I know that in the span of a few weeks, that defiantly pessimistic expression can be transformed into something beautiful: a look of love rediscovered, joy returned, and purpose restored. In fact, only four short weeks later, Jack and Alicia appeared to be more in love than they had ever been. They told me they could hardly believe the change.

What could possibly cause such a dramatic transformation? Nothing less than learning the secrets of what I call the *Exceptional Seven Percent,* those couples in first-and-forever marriages who exhibit much greater than average passion, happiness, longevity, and fulfillment in their relationships.

Mark and Jennifer have been married for nearly twenty years. Through good times and bad they have been able to maintain a partnership that is truly enviable. Mark says of his wife, "There isn't anybody who understands me as well as she does. I have friends at work and in the community, but there isn't anybody I'd rather be with than Jennifer—and she makes it pretty obvious that she feels the same about me. Sometimes my male friends kid me about how much time I spend with my wife. They think I don't go out with them after work because I'm afraid that I'll get in trouble or something. How ridiculous! They just don't get it, and I'm really not sure how to explain it to them. The reason I rush home at the end of the day is because Jennifer is my best friend—I mean, we share absolutely everything—and I genuinely miss her.

"Of course we have interests outside of our marriage and family life. Lots of things compete for our attention: the work we do, the causes we support, our community involvements....But everything else has to be secondary to our marriage because as far as we're concerned, the success of everything else depends on our ability to succeed as a couple."

What Planet Are These People From?

While it is uplifting to hear the stories of those who are happily married, the knowledge that exceptional couples like Mark and Jennifer exist leaves us with several important questions. For example, if less-than-exceptional marriages are made up of men from Mars and women from Venus, what planet do *these* couples come from? What do Exceptional couples know that others don't, and, more important, can what they know be taught? To begin to answer these questions, let's take a brief look at some of the research on exceptional couples.

In 1968, Dr. Don Jackson and William Lederer of the Palo Alto Mental Research Institute wrote a book called *The Mirages of Marriage.* In it, they identified a group of couples they called "collaborative geniuses" whose common backgrounds and "gracious stability" enabled them to be happier than average with each other over the years. The authors of the study suggested that only about 10 percent of all married couples fell into this, or similar, categories. However, Jackson and Lederer's description of such happy couples was purely theoretical and took up only two pages in their 450-page tome, thus demonstrating psychotherapy's traditional lack of interest in healthy people.

It was not until the mid-1990s that it was possible to say more about "exceptional" marriages based on observations of actual couples. At this time, sociologist Dr. Pepper Schwartz wrote a book called *Peer Marriage* that identified certain exceptional couples who exhibited traits like egalitarianism, a solidified value system, uncommon intimacy, deep friendship, and a unique commitment to their relationship. Around the same time, psychologist Dr. John Gottman wrote a book called *Why Marriages Succeed or Fail,* which described his fascinating longitudinal study of both healthy and unhealthy marriage behaviors. Remarkably, Dr. Gottman's study was able to predict, with 95 percent accuracy, which couples would be together and which couples would be divorced within five years. Even more importantly, data from his study strongly suggested that exceptional couples are made, not born.

Finally, psychologist Dr. Judith Wallerstein completed a critical examination of healthy marriages in her book, *The Good Marriage* (1995). In it she described a marital type called "Romantic Marriages," which I found to exhibit many traits strikingly similar to Dr. Schwartz's "peer couples." Dr. Wallerstein went on to state that 15 percent of the marriages she studied fell into this highly desirable category and about half of these—the group I call the Exceptional 7 Percent—were in first marriages.

Some cynics suggest that exceptional couples are "just born that way," but this is simply not the case. Dr. Gottman's study demonstrated that the difference between couples who were happy together and those who weren't boiled down to certain teachable skills, attitudes, and communication patterns. Further, Gottman's study is supported by Wallerstein's finding that half of all exceptional couples are in second marriages. In other words, if all exceptional couples were simply "born that way," half of them wouldn't have had to get divorced to figure out how to do it!

In my attempt to identify and explain what makes exceptional couples tick, I not only examined the relevant research on the subject, but I also thought about the couples I know personally and professionally who exhibit many of the traits these studies identified as being necessary for achieving exceptional status. I considered these couples with an eye toward identifying the rules they live by, the ways they think about their individual and married lives, and what habits, behaviors, or choices they demonstrated on a consistent basis that made them different from other good but somewhat less satisfying relationships.

Consider the following pages to be an orientation to the nine secrets of exceptional couples. As you read through each summary, complete the quizzes throughout the text. They will help direct you to the areas of your own marriage you should begin working on first. For best results, it will be necessary for both you and your mate to complete the quizzes. However, if for some reason your mate is unable to take the quizzes, you may attempt to answer for him or her. This is obviously a less desirable approach, but it is acceptable as long as you remember to be both fair in your answers and cautious in your interpretations of the final results.

The First Secret: A Marital Imperative

Every couple's marriage revolves around a theme, that thing to which a couple gives most of their time and emotional energy. For example, more conventional couples build their lives and marriages around either securing their basic needs, maintaining companionship and security, or finding each other's place in the world, investing heavily in careers or social roles. Exceptional couples, on the other hand, while concerned with all of these to some degree, spend most of their energy working together to pursue the development of positive character traits, moral virtue, and spiritual growth—a theme I call a marital imperative. In other words, exceptional couples consider their marriage to be their best hope for becoming the people they want to be at the end of their lives. This is the single most important way exceptional couples distinguish themselves. Their tendency to view marriage as a partnership in destiny accounts, in no small way, for the uncommon longevity and fulfillment these couples exhibit.

Take the following quiz to help you determine the clarity of your own marital imperative.

MARITAL IMPERATIVE QUIZ

Circle the level of agreement you have with each of the statements below. The points you receive for each item are printed below the answer you choose. Be honest. No one is going to see your results except you. Complete scoring and interpretive information will be presented later in the chapter.

a. I know the purpose of my life.

Strongly Disagree	Disagree	Undecided	Agree	Strongly Agree
1	2	3	4	5

b. My daily life and choices *obviously and consistently* reflect my attempt to fulfill the purpose of my life.

Strongly Disagree	Disagree	Undecided	Agree	Strongly Agree
1	2	3	4	5

c. My mate and I share *clearly defined* and compelling values, priorities, and ideals.

Strongly Disagree	Disagree	Undecided	Agree	Strongly Agree
1	2	3	4	5

d. Every day, my spouse and I consciously work to help each other live up to our clearly defined values, priorities, and ideals.

Strongly Disagree	Disagree	Undecided	Agree	Strongly Agree
1	2	3	4	5

e. I believe that my mate and I are *uniquely qualified* to help each other fulfill the purposes of our lives.

Strongly Disagree	Disagree	Undecided	Agree	Strongly Agree
1	2	3	4	5

You scored _____ out of a possible 25 points for this section.
Your mate scored _____ out of a possible 25 points for this section.
As a couple, you scored _____ out of a possible 50 points for Marital Imperative.

The Second Secret: Exceptional Fidelity

Most people think of fidelity in sexual terms, as in "I'm faithful because I'm not sleeping around," but exceptional couples have a broader understanding of this word. To them, fidelity, the promise to "forsake all others," includes all those friendships, family-of-origin commitments, career opportunities, and community involvements that do not serve to increase either the physical and mental health of each spouse or the intimacy of the marriage. This Exceptional Fidelity is absolutely essential if the marriage is to become a partnership in destiny (see the First Secret). That is not to say that Exceptional Fidelity requires a husband and wife to never leave the house. Rather, Exceptional Fidelity raises the couple to a new level. It empowers them to guard the initmate core of their marriage. It encourages them to prefer the meaningful companionship of a few close friends over a menagerie of casual acquaintances, and it dispels the illusion that social and occupational success must come at the price of marital poverty. Spouses in exceptional marriages don't give up anything that is truly important. They just don't waste time pursuing anything that isn't.

EXCEPTIONAL FIDELITY QUIZ

Circle the level of agreement you have with each of the statements below.

a. My work is *regularly* in competition with my marriage and family life.

Strongly Disagree	Disagree	Undecided	Agree	Strongly Agree
5	4	3	2	1

b. My social commitments or other friendships place many demands on me, sometimes making it difficult for me to find time for my marriage.

Strongly Disagree	Disagree	Undecided	Agree	Strongly Agree
5	4	3	2	1

c. Though I may feel guilty about it, I would often rather be at work or out with my friends than with my spouse.

Strongly Disagree	Disagree	Undecided	Agree	Strongly Agree
5	4	3	2	1

d. I feel caught in the middle between my parents and my spouse.

Strongly Disagree	Disagree	Undecided	Agree	Strongly Agree
5	4	3	2	1

e. When it comes to dividing up my time and energy, my marriage usually gets the leftovers.

Strongly Disagree	Disagree	Undecided	Agree	Strongly Agree
5	4	3	2	1

You scored _____ out of a possible 25 points for this section.
Your mate scored _____ out of a possible 25 points for this section.
As a couple, you scored _____ out of a possible 50 points for
Exceptional Fidelity.

The Third Secret: Exceptional Loving

To varying degrees, more conventional couples view love primarily as
a feeling, and they perform affectionate gestures when they *feel*
loving. Exceptional couples, on the other hand, view love as a calling.
They do loving things for their mate every day, whether or not they
feel like it and whether or not their mate "deserves" it. Why? For two
reasons. In the first place, it would be beneath their own personal
dignity to act any other way, and secondly, Exceptional couples know
that it is their personal commitment to being *actively* loving—
whether they feel like it or not—that helps them so often *feel* in love.
Loving behavior fuels loving emotions. Exceptional couples know this
and practice it.

EXCEPTIONAL LOVING QUIZ

Circle the level of agreement you have with each of the statements
below.

a. I believe it is possible for love to simply die.

Strongly Disagree	Disagree	Undecided	Agree	Strongly Agree
5	4	3	2	1

b. I think it is dishonest to do loving things for my mate if I don't feel
    lovingly toward him/her.

Strongly Disagree	Disagree	Undecided	Agree	Strongly Agree
5	4	3	2	1

c. I could easily answer the question, "What did you do today to
    show your mate how much you love him/her?"

Strongly Disagree	Disagree	Undecided	Agree	Strongly Agree
1	2	3	4	5

d. Love is either there or it isn't. Good relationships shouldn't ever
    feel like work.

Strongly Disagree	Disagree	Undecided	Agree	Strongly Agree
5	4	3	2	1

e. My mate regularly compliments me on how thoughtful and affectionate I am.

Strongly Disagree	Disagree	Undecided	Agree	Strongly Agree
1	2	3	4	5

You scored _____ out of a possible 25 points for this section.

Your mate scored _____ out of a possible 25 points for this section.

As a couple, you scored _____ out of a possible 50 points for Exceptional Loving.

The Fourth Secret: Exceptional Service

Exceptional couples value daily, mutual service more than "fairness" or sharply defined roles and responsibilities. To put it another way, Exceptional couples do not argue over turf issues. Also, because neither the husband nor the wife views the marriage license as a permission slip granting either of them the right to sit around waiting to be taken care of, each actively looks for opportunities to serve and nurture their mate, creating a *dance of competence* that enables chores and other domestic responsibilities to be passed back and forth gracefully, and accomplished efficiently. For example:

Q: In an Exceptional marriage, who dusts the table?

A: Whoever bumps into it first.

For the Exceptional couple this attitude is a common thread throughout every aspect of work, family, and domestic life. While more conventional couples view service as a means to an end (When I do nice things, I get affection/appreciation in return; when I don't get appreciation/affection, I stop doing nice things), Exceptional couples view service as an end in itself (When I do nice things I am exercising and fulfilling the values with which I most closely identify; service is its own reward). I am not suggesting that Exceptional couples don't appreciate being appreciated—in fact, they give and receive more expressions of gratitude than most couples (see The Seventh Secret)—it is simply that applause is not their primary motivator, and they recognize that emotional scorekeeping or maneuvering to see who takes better care of whom are fruitless exercises.

EXCEPTIONAL SERVICE QUIZ

Circle the level of agreement you have with each of the statements below.

a. All day long, I look for opportunities to make my mate's life easier or more pleasant.

Strongly Disagree	Disagree	Undecided	Agree	Strongly Agree
1	2	3	4	5

b. Every day, it is obvious to me that my mate looks for opportunities to make my life easier or more pleasant.

Strongly Disagree	Disagree	Undecided	Agree	Strongly Agree
1	2	3	4	5

c. Frequently and cheerfully, I do household jobs that are not specifically "mine" to do.

Strongly Disagree	Disagree	Undecided	Agree	Strongly Agree
1	2	3	4	5

d. Frequently and cheerfully, my mate does household jobs that are not specifically his/hers to do.

Strongly Disagree	Disagree	Undecided	Agree	Strongly Agree
1	2	3	4	5

e. My mate would agree with me if I made the following statement: "I am good at remembering and anticipating my spouse's needs."

Strongly Disagree	Disagree	Undecided	Agree	Strongly Agree
1	2	3	4	5

You scored _____ out of a possible 25 points for this section.

Your mate scored _____ out of a possible 25 points for this section.

As a couple, you scored _____ out of a possible 50 points for Exceptional Service.

The Fifth Secret: Exceptional Rapport

Research clearly shows that Exceptional couples are equal partners in their capacity for emotional and verbal expression. Because of their willingness to be challenged and grow, men and women in Exceptional marriages have learned to overcome both their basic gender and personality differences, allowing them to achieve an enviable level of understanding and rapport in their relationships.

EXCEPTIONAL RAPPORT QUIZ

Circle the level of agreement you have with each of the statements below.

a. Sometimes it seems like my mate and I are speaking two different languages.

Strongly Disagree	Disagree	Undecided	Agree	Strongly Agree
5	4	3	2	1

b. I often feel like something is missing in my marriage, but I don't know what.

Strongly Disagree	Disagree	Undecided	Agree	Strongly Agree
5	4	3	2	1

c. I often feel that my mate *does not* understand me.

Strongly Disagree	Disagree	Undecided	Agree	Strongly Agree
5	4	3	2	1

d. Sometimes I think my mate *does not* understand what it takes to have a good relationship.

Strongly Disagree	Disagree	Undecided	Agree	Strongly Agree
5	4	3	2	1

e. My mate and I are both good at expressing our love for each other.

Strongly Disagree	Disagree	Undecided	Agree	Strongly Agree
1	2	3	4	5

You scored _____ out of a possible 25 points for this section.

Your mate scored _____ out of a possible 25 points for this section.

As a couple, you scored _____ out of a possible 50 points for Exceptional Rapport.

The Sixth Secret: Exceptional Negotiation

Arguments between less satisfied husbands and wives tend to look like competitions to see whose need will be met this time. For such couples, fairness is determined by having an equal score in the game of giving-in. But in Exceptional relationships, all needs are respected and met—even when a partner's need is not completely understood. That your need will be met is never called into question; the only topic of debate is, "What is the most efficient, respectful means by which your need can be met ?"

Simply put, Exceptional couples live by the following rule: Never negotiate the "what." Always negotiate the "how" and "when."

EXCEPTIONAL NEGOTIATION QUIZ

Circle the level of agreement you have with each of the statements below.

a. When my mate and I have a disagreement, it feels like we are competing to see whose need or agenda is "more important"—or who has more power.

Strongly Disagree	Disagree	Undecided	Agree	Strongly Agree
5	4	3	2	1

b. Even when my mate and I strongly disagree, I feel like (s)he makes an effort to respect and understand my needs and opinions.

Strongly Disagree	Disagree	Undecided	Agree	Strongly Agree
1	2	3	4	5

c. Sometimes I suspect that my mate gives up his/her own needs rather than tell me what (s)he thinks and risks continuing an argument.

Strongly Disagree	Disagree	Undecided	Agree	Strongly Agree
5	4	3	2	1

d. I would rather surrender my own need than risk continuing an argument.

Strongly Disagree	Disagree	Undecided	Agree	Strongly Agree
5	4	3	2	1

e. I frequently feel demeaned/demoralized after a disagreement with my mate.

Strongly Disagree	Disagree	Undecided	Agree	Strongly Agree
5	4	3	2	1

You scored _____ out of a possible 25 points for this section.

Your mate scored _____ out of a possible 25 points for this section.

As a couple, you scored _____ out of a possible 50 points for Exceptional Negotiation.

The Seventh Secret: Exceptional Gratitude

In exceptional marriages, every service—no matter how common or simple—is viewed as an active expression of love to be noted and appreciated. Because the level of mutual service is so high (see the Fourth Secret), there are no real expectations about the chores one's mate has to do to "keep up their end." Yes, dinner must be cooked, bills must be paid, kids must be picked up, and homes must be cleaned, but, "You didn't have to do it." This view is absolutely essential if true gratitude is to flourish. Anything less, and gratitude gives way to expectation ("Why should I thank you, it's your job to do that!") or self-righteous scorekeeping ("I did all this for you and you couldn't even...").

Exceptional couples tend to say thank you for "silly" or "common" things for which more conventional couples would never think of voicing appreciation.

EXCEPTIONAL GRATITUDE QUIZ

Circle the level of agreement you have with each of the statements below.

a. I know that my mate appreciates me and all I do.

Strongly Disagree	Disagree	Undecided	Agree	Strongly Agree
1	2	3	4	5

b. Every day, I look for opportunities to compliment or thank my mate.

Strongly Disagree	Disagree	Undecided	Agree	Strongly Agree
1	2	3	4	5

c. I am good at noticing and complimenting changes my mate makes in his/her appearance.

Strongly Disagree	Disagree	Undecided	Agree	Strongly Agree
1	2	3	4	5

d. I am good at noticing and complimenting the things my mate does to maintain our home or to improve it.

Strongly Disagree	Disagree	Undecided	Agree	Strongly Agree
1	2	3	4	5

e. I couldn't imagine a partner better suited to me than my mate.

Strongly Disagree	Disagree	Undecided	Agree	Strongly Agree
1	2	3	4	5

You scored _____ out of a possible 25 points for this section.
Your mate scored _____ out of a possible 25 points for this section.
As a couple, you scored _____ out of a possible 50 points for Exceptional Gratitude.

The Eighth Secret: Exceptional Joy

Part of the Exceptional couple's strength is their ability to play and be joyful together. They look for new interests to share and work to share in the interests they already have. They are comfortable being silly together. They know which areas of their partner's life are acceptable teasing material and which are off-limits. They make time to be together, work at being present to each other, and actively seek ways to ease each other's burdens. Compare this to more conventional couples who used to play together, "but who has time now?" Or other husbands and wives who are forced to develop separate interests and friendships because their spouse frequently greets invitations to certain activities with, "You know I don't enjoy doing *that!*"

EXCEPTIONAL JOY QUIZ

Circle the level of agreement you have with each of the statements below.

a. I enjoy spending time with my mate more than with anyone else.

Strongly Disagree	Disagree	Undecided	Agree	Strongly Agree
1	2	3	4	5

b. If it came down to a choice, I would rather be doing something I didn't enjoy *with* my mate, than something I did enjoy *without* my mate.

Strongly Disagree	Disagree	Undecided	Agree	Strongly Agree
1	2	3	4	5

c. I am comfortable with the way, and the degree to which, my mate and I tease each other.

Strongly Disagree	Disagree	Undecided	Agree	Strongly Agree
1	2	3	4	5

d. My mate and I share a lot of laughs and good times.

Strongly Disagree	Disagree	Undecided	Agree	Strongly Agree
1	2	3	4	5

e. My mate knows just what to do to uplift me when I am going through a difficult time.

Strongly Disagree	Disagree	Undecided	Agree	Strongly Agree
1	2	3	4	5

You scored _____ out of a possible 25 points for this section.

Your mate scored _____ out of a possible 25 points for this section.

As a couple, you scored _____ out of a possible 50 points for Exceptional Joy.

The Ninth Secret: Exceptional Sexuality

Exceptional couples have developed a truly spiritual, life-giving sexuality. More conventional couples view sex as something they do, another activity—albeit a pleasant one—that they just don't have the time and energy for very often. But Exceptional couples view sex as something they *are*. Every quality discussed in this book, from mutual service to fidelity, from love to joy and everything in between is represented and practiced in the lovemaking of the exceptional couple. For them, lovemaking is not an activity or a performance; it is a total self-gift, a symbol and expression of all that is good about themselves and their relationship. Where the conventional couple can feel pressured by the responsibility of maintaining their sex life, Exceptional couples draw strength from their sex life (which is a reflection of their marriage as a whole) to allow them to deal with the stress of things less fascinating than their marriage.

EXCEPTIONAL SEXUALITY QUIZ

Circle the level of agreement you have with each of the statements below.

a. Lovemaking *regularly* gets put off due to stress or exhaustion.

Strongly Disagree	Disagree	Undecided	Agree	Strongly Agree
5	4	3	2	1

b. I feel like my mate makes love to my mind and spirit, not just my body.

Strongly Disagree	Disagree	Undecided	Agree	Strongly Agree
1	2	3	4	5

c. I think of lovemaking as both a renewal of our wedding vows and a celebration of all that is good in our marriage.

Strongly Disagree	Disagree	Undecided	Agree	Strongly Agree
1	2	3	4	5

d. I consider children to be a great blessing and I think my mate is (would be) an exceptional parent.

Strongly Disagree	Disagree	Undecided	Agree	Strongly Agree
1	2	3	4	5

e. I am comfortable with any and all of the following: making love with the lights on, telling my mate what pleases me and what doesn't, trying new positions, laughing during sex, and both verbally and physically expressing my pleasure during lovemaking.

Strongly Disagree	Disagree	Undecided	Agree	Strongly Agree
1	2	3	4	5

You scored _____ out of a possible 25 points for this section.
Your mate scored _____ out of a possible 25 points for this section.
As a couple, you scored _____ out of a possible 50 points for Exceptional Sexuality.

Developing Your Action Plan

In this section, you will identify both the strengths and opportunities for growth your marriage presents. By the end of this exercise, you will have a good idea of what you need to do to help your marriage better resemble those of the Exceptional 7 Percent. Because each marriage is different, every couple will score differently overall, and every couple will be better at certain skills than others. Try not to look at the quizzes as simply picking out your weak points. Rather, concentrate on the things you *are* good at, and build from there.

Sometimes people get a little paranoid about what the results of self-help quizzes actually mean. Please note that the self-tests included in this book are not scientifically validated instruments. Scoring low on a particular quiz—or even a number of quizzes—does not necessarily mean that your marriage is bad, and scoring high on them doesn't necessarily mean your marriage is exceptional. What your score does point to is how much loving attention your marriage needs in order for it to become all that you want it to be. That said, let's look at how you scored overall.

Go back through the last several pages and, in the spaces provided, write the scores you each received individually and as a couple for each trait discussed.

	You	Your Mate	Couple
1. Marital Imperative	_____	_____	_____
2. Fidelity	_____	_____	_____
3. Love	_____	_____	_____
4. Service	_____	_____	_____
5. Rapport	_____	_____	_____
6. Negotiation	_____	_____	_____
7. Gratitude	_____	_____	_____
8. Joy	_____	_____	_____
9. Sexuality	_____	_____	_____

As a couple, you and your mate scored _____ out of a possible 450 points.

Keeping in mind that this is not a scientifically validated instrument, it has been my experience that Exceptional couples tend to score in the 420+ range. Please remember, these couples—being part of the Exceptional 7 Percent—would be expected to score higher than 93 percent of all other couples in first marriages (and 85 percent of all couples). If you did not score in this range it does not mean your marriage is bad. For example, scoring in the 360+ range is still very respectable—a bit like getting a solid B or B+. Couples scoring in this comparatively lower range still have some of the best marriages on the block. And if you scored lower than this, it *still* doesn't mean your marriage is bad. It simply suggests that you may have been taking either your mate or your marriage more for granted than you ought to and, if this is the case, you've come to the right place.

The reason I feel the need to tell you over and over how good your marriage probably is, is that this book has an entirely different focus than most self-help books. Other self-help books are interested in telling the reader how to take a rotten relationship and make it passable. While *The Exceptional Seven Percent* could be used in this manner, most of the information contained in these pages would be lost on a truly miserable couple. The main focus of *The Exceptional Seven Percent* is to show couples how to take an average to good relationship and turn it into something profound, blissful, and energizing. Please keep this in mind as you work through the remainder of the book.

Now, let's take a look at your particular strengths and weaknesses.

Review your individual scores to each quiz. In the space provided below, write the three areas you and your mate scored highest in, individually.

You scored highest in...   *Your mate scored highest in...*

1. _____ 1. _____

2. _____ 2. _____

3. _____ 3. _____

These areas represent your and your mate's unique strengths, respectively. Over the next few days, discuss how you will share your particular strengths with each other. For example, how could you help your mate develop more of a particular quality? How could your mate do the same for you? What are the struggles you expect to encounter as you attempt to increase your proficiency in a particular area? What struggles will your mate face? Take time with these questions and discuss them thoroughly.

As a rule of thumb, if you scored higher than your partner on a specific trait, it will be your responsibility to help your mate grow in that area, and vice versa. I do not mean to suggest that a lower-scoring spouse has to do everything the "expert" in a particular area says to do. But I would invite the spouse who scores lower to give serious consideration to any gently and charitably offered suggestions his or her higher scoring mate might make on improving a particular trait.

Now let's look at the areas that you will want to improve upon as a couple.

Review the couple's scores you received on each quiz. In the space provided below, write the three areas that as a couple you and your mate scored the lowest in.

As a couple, we need to improve in these three areas.

1. _____

2. _____

3. _____

These represent the areas on which you and your mate will want to focus most of your attention as you begin your journey toward Exceptional couplehood. Of course you should feel free to discuss these areas now, but I will defer any particular discussion questions and tips until later. Just be sure to pay particular attention to these chapters as you read through the book and you will receive many helpful suggestions for increasing the frequency of these positive traits in your marriage.

The Circle of Intimacy

As you consider the nine secrets, it will most likely be obvious to you how each of the Exceptional couple's qualities, attitudes, and behaviors play off of each other in an ever-widening circle of intimacy, devotion, and actualization (that is, being a living, breathing example of your values, ideals, and goals). Couples who practice these secrets in their marriages are able to tap into the true transformative power of love. They become each other's best hope of arriving at the end of their lives as the people they always wanted to grow up to be.

For some of you, the ideal that is the Exceptional marriage might seem somehow unrealistic. Our disposable culture has taught us to believe that transformative love is the stuff of fairy tales, but nothing could be further from the truth. From the very beginning, we humans were built to love, to be loved, and to be transformed by love. As infants, we fail to thrive if we are not loved, touched, cuddled, and nurtured—rejecting even food if our greater hunger for affection remains unsatisfied. It could very easily be claimed, on biological and physiological grounds, that we are hard-wired for intimacy from the very first day of life. It is true that somewhere along the way many adults lose the innate instruction manual that would teach them how to satisfy this most deep-seated of needs, but there is good news. With proper training and a willing heart, we can learn to love and be loved as we were created to. No matter where your relationship stands today, you must take comfort and encouragement from the fact that you and your mate were born with the ability to celebrate Exceptional love in your lives and—by association—in your marriage. By practicing the secrets of the Exceptional 7 Percent, you will discover that the path to Exceptional love lies within you, because Exceptional love is your innate call; it is the essential ground of your physical, emotional, and spiritual being. It is what you were built to do.

So, turn the page, and let's get to it.

2

The Relationship Pathway

*The relation between any two decently married people
changes profoundly every few years... every change
causes pain, even if it brings a certain joy. Marriage is
a long event of perpetual change in which a man and
a woman mutually build up their souls and make
themselves whole.*

—D. H. LAWRENCE

WHY ARE you married?

Your answer to this question has everything to do with the
longevity, happiness, and fulfillment you can expect from your
relationship. While there are many possible responses, they all break
down into discernible categories or themes, if you will, which guide
the overall course of the marriage. For example some couples build
their marriage around the theme of escape, hoping to use each other
to avoid dealing with a world which they believe is either too
overwhelming or too uninteresting. Other couples build their lives
around achieving their basic needs, attempting to guarantee financial
or emotional security for themselves—often at the expense of true

intimacy or love. For most conventional couples, the primary motivation for marriage is companionship, cheering each other on as both partners seek their place in the world at large. Finally, there are those Exceptional couples who construct their marriages around fulfilling a marital imperative, a deeply held, clearly defined set of values, ideals, and goals. Over the next few pages, you will become more aware of the advantages and disadvantages of your own marital theme and discover the incredible benefits of building your relationship around a marital imperative, the only theme which all but guarantees the lifelong relevance, happiness, and success of a marriage.

That different marriages revolve around different themes is a fairly well established fact, but to date, no one has been able to show a meaningful connection among these themes. For example, based on available research, a marriage therapist could probably identify your marriage as, let's say, a "blue marriage" and likewise tell you that it was not as desirable as a "green marriage." But the same therapist would be hardpressed to tell you exactly how to move from your marriage into the more desirable one except perhaps to suggest that you need to "communicate better" or, "hope for better luck the next time you marry." Until now, there was simply no meaningful way to tell couples what specific issues they needed to address to move to the next, more satisfying, stage of their lives together.

The Relationship Pathway is a model I have developed to explain how marital themes (and, in turn, marital satisfaction) can evolve over the life of a marriage. The Relationship Pathway illustrates the skills, attitudes, and behaviors a couple must learn in order to move from one major marital type to another. Further, it suggests that most marriages are basically good and can likewise become exceptional if a couple takes the time to learn what to do and practice what they know.

The Relationship Pathway (Figure 2.1) organizes five major categories of marriage (and a few subtypes) along a continuum of identity strength. (Readers with some psychology background may note the correspondence between the Relationship Pathway and Abraham Maslow's "Hierarchy of Needs.") Each marital type on the pathway is rated as being Impoverished, Conventional, or Exceptional, and as a couple moves up the pathway, the potential for marital happiness and longevity increases. Though every couple starts out at a different point on the Relationship Pathway, they all move along it one stage at a

The Relationship Pathway

*Every relationship travels left to right from its starting point on **The Relationship Pathway**. As couples meet new challenges and learn new skills, both their identity strength and marital satisfaction increase.*

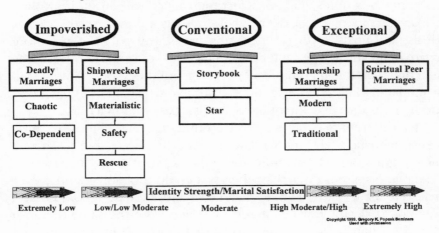

Figure 2.1

time. There is no skipping grades because not only does each stage of the pathway represent a shift in relational attitudes and the mastery of different skills, but each stage also reflects a change in the way the couple view their whole life. As such, it often takes a major crisis—the kind that makes us say, "I don't know anything, anymore"—to motivate us to make the personal changes necessary to move from one relationship stage to the next. A person can move up the pathway without going through such a crisis, but he would have to be seriously and consistently attentive to his psychological and marital growth. Frankly, most of us are too lazy and distracted to do this, and it takes our lives falling apart before we are willing to take the steps necessary to move toward greater identity strength and deeper intimacy with our mate.

As you search for your own marriage on the pathway, try to keep the following in mind. First of all, resist the temptation to canonize yourself while demonizing your mate. Some people try to place themselves at the top of the pathway and their mate at the bottom: This is not the way it works. We all marry people whose identities are built around similar things to our own. Chances are, if you married a rotten apple, you're not so shiny yourself.

24

Also, because it takes so much energy to move from one stage to the next, and because these stages are organized along a continuum, don't be surprised if you find yourself between two stages. Most people are. Simply choose the stage or marital theme with which you most closely identify and start working on the recommendations listed in that section first, even if all the specifics don't apply.

In order to help you understand the progression from one stage to the next, we'll start at the bottom and work our way up.

Impoverished Marriages

Impoverished marriages get their name from the lower levels of intimacy, satisfaction, and longevity couples in them experience. The two major marital types that fall under the Impoverished rating are Deadly marriages and Shipwrecked marriages.

Deadly Marriages

MARITAL THEME: Escape from a world that is perceived as being either too overwhelming or too uninteresting to deal with.

In the Impoverished marriage category, the first stop is the Deadly marriage. A Deadly marriage occurs when two people build their lives around a self-destructive attempt to escape the world, which they have deemed either too overwhelming or too uninteresting to deal with. Deadly marriages come in two varieties: the Chaotic marriage and the Codependent marriage.

The Chaotic marriage exists when two people, equally bent on their own self-destruction (think of the movie *Leaving Las Vegas*), get together and become each other's drinking buddies, sex partners, and possibly, punching bags. This couple is content to have just enough money to numb themselves through their day. These relationships rarely last, nor should they. If they do, it is often because one person (usually the woman) fears that leaving would jeopardize her life. The only way to have a worse marriage is to marry a serial killer, but the good news is you can really only go up from here.

A Codependent marriage exists when one person (it is usually a man), bent on his own self-destruction, marries someone (usually a woman) who intends to save him from himself. "Codependent" is probably the most overused word in pop psychology, and in the popular culture it has come to mean anyone who does anything for someone else that she really doesn't want to do. This is unfortunate because it blunts the true, insidious nature of codependence.

Perhaps an example would help explain what I mean. Some people enjoy watching soap operas because, for an hour or so, they can forget about their own problems and lose themselves in the entertainingly hopeless problems of the characters on-screen. The true codependent person lives her entire life this way. The codependent has a whole laundry list of personal problems from which she distracts herself by becoming involved with someone whose daily existence is a life-or-death drama. The logic goes like this: "I can't solve my own problems, so I will save this unsavable person, after which, he can save me." Perverse as this may sound to any normal person, for the codependent this logic represents a win-win opportunity. Either the crazy prophecy will come true and the unsavable person will save her (this never happens) or the unsavable person continues to be hopeless, providing endless hours of wonderful, heroic distraction from the codependent's own problems. Codependent marriages tend to exhibit a fairly high degree of longevity (due to the codependent's tenacity) although, understandably, they are extremely unsatisfactory for the couple.

Recommendations for Deadly Couples

Relationships in the Deadly category are the only marriages which research strongly and consistently suggests would be better off dissolved. But if a Chaotic or Codependent couple wishes to remain together, they will have to accomplish one major mental shift (besides sobriety) before they can hope to move to the next marital stage (the Shipwrecked marriage). Specifically, they will have to learn to demand at least basic safety and basic financial security from their lives and relationships. Depending upon the specifics of the couple, AA, Al-Anon, and individual psychotherapy may all be indicated. Marital therapy per se is useless at this stage because there are barely two whole, functioning people here, much less a marriage.

Now let's examine the next marriage type on the pathway, the Shipwrecked marriage. Though this type also falls into the Impoverished category, it is a breath of fresh air compared to the relationships you just read about.

Shipwrecked Marriages

MARITAL THEME: Providing the basics (financial security; safety and quietude) needed for a "comfortable life."

Shipwrecked marriages represent the second stage of the Relationship Pathway. Once people become convinced that they cannot escape life, they begin to learn how to meet their basic needs. This is the primary work, the marital theme, of the Shipwrecked marriage.

The identities of husbands and wives in Shipwrecked marriages are still in their infancy. Lacking a solid sense of self, they use each other and their relationship to define themselves. Essentially, Shipwrecked husbands and wives view the world as a stormy sea into which they were cast with only the driftwood of their marriage to keep them afloat—hence the name. Shipwrecked couples either married too young to know they could expect more from life beyond the basics or were raised in homes where their material and safety needs were never guaranteed. Because of this, they distinguish themselves by how much of their lives revolve around pursuing the basic needs of life (financial security; safety). While all couples desire and even need these things, Shipwrecked couples never seem to know when enough is enough. They are either constantly pursuing more and more financial security or working to lead quieter and more stress-free lives until there is nothing left except the pursuit of these most basic of goals.

Shipwrecked marriages usually deteriorate into "brother and sister" relationships through the years because they are not so much founded on love as they are on functionality: paying bills, maintaining the house, raising the children. Likewise, the basic differences between men and women are most keenly felt here. Shipwrecked husbands and wives spend a great deal of time staring at each other saying, "I don't understand what the hell you want from me. Why do you have to be such a (wo)man?"

Historically, Shipwrecked marriages lasted a lifetime, though they were less than happy. In the present day, due to both the loss of the divorce taboo and the social and career opportunities available for women, they tend to have an approximate lifespan of ten years (including any years of premarital cohabitation).

The set of basics which are most important to a couple will determine to which of the three types of Shipwrecked marriages they belong: Materialistic, Safety, or Rescue. We will take a brief look at each.

The Materialistic marriage values financial security above all else. This can translate into either the obsessive pursuit of wealth, an extreme level of frugality, or both. Materialistic marriages tend to have a traditional structure and the roles of the husband and wife are defined in an extremely rigid manner. Compliance with these roles is strictly enforced. The husband in a Materialistic marriage may or may not have an important, well-paying, or glamorous career, but regardless, he does not gain satisfaction from his work so much as he gains satisfaction from the money he makes or the power and esteem his work may win him. Being thought of as a "great guy" is very important to the Materialistic husband who builds his life around overcompensating for his basic insecurities. He is the person everybody likes, but when you think about it, has no close friends. (Tom Cruise's character in the movie *Jerry Maguire* is a good example of a man moving through the Materialistic stage of a relationship.) He is often gregarious with everyone except his family, toward whom he is either neglectful or abusive. He also tends to be fairly jealous, possessive, and controlling with his wife. The wife, on the other hand, fears more than anything else that she would be unable to provide for herself in the manner to which she has become accustomed. Because she feels unqualified for any other work, the role of wife and mother has fallen to her. Though she says she loves her children, this love may be mixed with a fair dose of resentment because she often feels trapped by her life. This is the housewife who has been said to lead a life of "quiet desperation."

Both husband and wife are extremely dependent upon each other. As previously mentioned, the Materialistic wife is dependent upon the husband for her financial needs and social standing. The Materialistic husband, on the other hand, is dependent upon his wife to uphold his fragile ego and legitimize him ("I'm married. I can't be all bad"). His dependency on her is not quite as obvious on a day-to-day basis, but it comes out in force if she ever tries to leave him. At such a time he will either make overblown promises to change everything in his life that offends her (though he would be hard pressed to identify those things) or, failing at this approach, he may threaten suicide or homicide ("If you leave me, I'll kill myself. Who knows, I might just take you with me!").

Around the ten-year mark, many wives in Materialistic marriages strike a blow for independence. This is often precipitated by the wife either finding a way to meet her own financial needs or taking a new lover on whom she can lean. The marriage rarely survives such a blow. Those couples who do not receive competent counseling but somehow make it beyond this crisis phase will remain stable— though depressed—until the children are grown, after which the marriage may be threatened with another war for independence.

The second type of Shipwrecked marriage is the Safety marriage, which is at the other end of the spectrum. Safety marriages occur when a woman who has had a deprived or traumatic past marries a nice, quiet man who will not threaten her. The main theme of this marriage is safety, in the form of avoiding conflict and pursuing a completely stress-free life. By her choice of a husband, the wife is assured that any arguments are likely to be on her terms, although she is usually just as happy to remain quiet because, "Life is too short to fight." The couple tends to have more than their share of financial problems—they are hardly the corporate killer types—although wives in these marriages are more likely to be employed out of the home (usually from necessity). Also, because of the wife's influence, they are more likely to be churchgoers than their Materialistic counterparts, though their faith tends to be shallow, celebrating either feel-good spiritual vagaries or rigid religiosity.

This relationship goes along just fine until about ten years into the marriage when the wife finally becomes sated with safety and quietude and expresses a desire for more passion in her life and marriage. Unfortunately, she discovers that the same man who could not threaten her also lacks the skills and motivation to love her as well as she would now like. From this point on, there will be tension in the marriage—though it may not be voiced—as the wife drags her husband to therapy, church, support groups, anything that will "fix" him, and get her the husband that she needs. Even when it works, it is a painfully slow process.

Finally, the Shipwrecked Rescue marriage is the more satisfying hybrid of the two Shipwrecked marriages you have just read about. Identified by Dr. Judith Wallerstein in her book, *The Good Marriage* (1995), both the husband and wife in a Rescue marriage usually come from severely neglectful, abusive, or deprived families of origin. But unlike other Shipwrecked couples who eventually come to desire more intimacy or greater identity strength (thus inviting the tension that either propels them toward the next stage on the pathway or destroys the marriage), Rescue couples are just happy to have survived their traumatic pasts and never learn to ask for anything more from life. As one Rescue wife told me, "I suppose I love him. Not like *most* people mean it, but, you know....He doesn't beat me. He doesn't drink too much or sleep around. He makes a good living. What do I have to complain about?"

Despite the relative "satisfaction" of Rescue couples, these marriages belong in the Impoverished category because they are still only about achieving the basics in life, are still seriously lacking in intimacy, still exhibit unhealthy levels of mutual dependency, still depend upon lives that are too sheltered from the world at large, and—generally speaking—are not marriages that anyone with a healthy upbringing would aspire to.

Recommendations for Shipwrecked Couples

In order for Shipwrecked couples to move to the next step on the pathway (Conventional marriages), they need to look at the following in their lives.

1. *Expect more from life.* If you are in a Shipwrecked marriage, you have learned that it was either foolish or selfish to want more than "the basics" from life. To a large degree, this is what caused you to create a marriage that resembles the alien houseplant in the musical *Little Shop of Horrors.* That is, it sucks the life out of you to sustain itself. A healthy marriage is not a drain; it is a life-giving thing that empowers you to become the person you were created to be. The first step toward this marital ideal is to stop thinking of your dreams, goals, ideals, and values as something to take up one day after you win the lottery. Finding work or roles that are personally meaningful—as opposed to merely practical, well-paying, or even important—is essential to entering the next stage of your identity development and married life.

2. *Learn to meet your own needs.* In order for love to blossom in your marriage, you have to rout out your dependency. What do you rely on your mate to do for you that, at this point, you are unable or unwilling to do for yourself? Earn a living? Clean house? Cook? Discipline your children? Make friends? Feel good about yourself? Get

the training, practice, or counseling you need to overcome your neediness, because need chokes off love.

3. *Relate to your mate.* Shipwrecked spouses spend far too much time standing around wondering what their mate wants from them. You have no excuse for this. Books like John Gray's Mars and Venus series, Gary Smalley's *Hidden Keys to a Loving, Lasting Marriage,* or Deborah Tannen's *You Just Don't Understand,* and programs like Promise Keepers , PAIRS, or Retrouvaille, etc., were meant for you. Take advantage of them. Also, seek individual or marriage counseling to help you be accountable for the changes you want to make.

4. *Challenge your addiction to comfort.* If you have a chaotic past, you may feel you are now entitled a bit of peace and quiet. Unfortunately, this may make you obstinately unwilling to give any more to your mate than *you* decide is necessary. You may be blatantly dismissive toward, or passively ignoring of, your mate's requests for more time, more attention, more anything. Likewise, you may tend to nag your mate about his or her faults as a way to escape dealing with your own. Both are recipes for disaster. If you wanted comfort, you should have bought a lounge chair, not a marriage license. Get to work on fulfilling your and your mate's destinies now.

If you are currently in a Shipwrecked marriage, I want to encourage you to do the work necessary to move to the next stage. The crisis these marriages encounter around the ten-year mark is not so much an interpersonal problem as it is an identity problem. Stop blaming your mate for your misery and begin working to find your own place in the world. Your mate may disapprove of your efforts, but in many ways, this is just the tension your psyche requires to build some identity strength. Let your spouse be the stone against which you sharpen the sword of your identity. For now, let your marriage meet your basic needs while you pursue your growth. In the meantime, try to encourage your spouse to grow as well. If he or she does, great. If not, then you can reevaluate your decision to stay in your marriage *after* you have achieved a position of greater personal, social, and financial strength.

The next stage on the Relationship Pathway accounts for most marriages and represents what the Shipwrecked couple will graduate to if they successfully complete the work I outlined above.

Conventional Marriages

The marital theme of a Conventional marriage is generally to support and maintain a couple's place in the world. Once people are capable of meeting their own basic needs, they become interested in finding a group with which they can identify and they are ready for a Conventional marriage. Even though Conventional couples exhibit some of the same qualities, attitudes, and skills as those couples farther along the pathway, they have not yet mastered them. Depending upon how the couples marital theme is played out, the Conventional couples will find themselves in either a Storybook or a Star marriage. Basic requirements for admission into either type of Conventional marriage are as follows.

1. Both husband and wife must be relatively sure of their own ability to provide for at least their basic financial needs, even if they are not currently employed.

2. Both husband and wife must have found personally meaningful work or social roles to play. For example, a physician whose identity is in the Shipwrecked category enjoys medicine because of the money, power, and prestige her work affords her, while a physician whose identity is at least in the Conventional category truly enjoys the art of medicine. In a similar way, to qualify as a Conventional stay-at-home mom (as opposed to a Shipwrecked stay-at-home mom), the woman must sincerely believe that by training or experience she is qualified to do something else, but has chosen to stay home because she finds the role personally meaningful and socially valuable.

3. Both husband and wife must have at least a casual identification with, or membership in, some significant "values group"; for example, church or synagogue, professional organizations, political/community organizations, men's/women's groups. Such identifications are important because, as Abraham Maslow pointed out, being accepted by and belonging to the world at large is a necessary step on the road to actualization. Likewise, analyst Erik Erikson showed how identification with some form of values group (even a conflicted identification) is a necessary part of developing healthy identity strength.

The Conventional husband and wife will use their membership or identification with such groups to sharpen their self-concept, clarifying the values that are important to them (although "values" at this stage tends to mean a particular political/social agenda rather than a marital imperative or a personal mission or code). Much of the Conventional couple's involvement in their respective groups will involve the husband or wife comparing themselves to other members in the group to see how they measure up, a kind of psychosocial "keeping up with the Joneses." This activity plants the seeds of accountability in the marriage ("I'm at least as good a spouse as so-and-so is.") which, if allowed to blossom, will be the most important catalyst for moving the couple to the next stage on the pathway.

4. Both the husband and wife must have negotiated at least the most basic communication differences between men and women. Conventional couples may occasionally fall into that "it's a guy thing" or "it's a girl thing" trap, but this is the exception, not the rule as with Shipwrecked couples.

These are the most important attributes distinguishing Conventional marriages from their Shipwrecked counterparts, who are still struggling to figure out what to do with themselves apart from their marriage, and tend to have a mildly paranoid, self-protective attitude toward the world at large, especially organized groups.

Conventional marriages are the first relationships on the pathway that are founded on love. The love here is warm and comfortable, though the degree of intimacy can be a bit shallow due to the Conventional husband and wife's tendency to get lost in their own little worlds and do not attend enough to their marriage. In fact, the ultimate success of the Conventional marriage is dependent upon the couple's ability to maintain their priorities and perspective. Doing this will prevent the number one threat to Conventional marriages: "growing apart." (See chapters 5 and 7.)

Besides growing apart, the other two problems that all types of Conventional couples encounter are domestic scorekeeping (whose turn is it to do what chore or how much of a contribution is a "fair" contribution to the marriage), and a game I call marital chicken. Marital chicken is reminiscent of the old game of chicken played in cars, in which two people drive toward each other at high speeds in an attempt to see who veers off first. Marital chicken is played when a husband or wife says, "I *would* be more romantic/sexual/attentive/helpful/emotional/reasonable if you would only be more romantic/sexual/attentive/helpful/emotional/reasonable, but I know you, you'll never change." Marital chicken serves the dual function of excusing spouses from changing anything about themselves while allowing each to feel self-righteous at the same time. As you might guess, marital chicken can be addicting.

Conventional couples are susceptible to these games because, though they have a fair amount of identity strength, their identities can be said to be more in their adolescence. As such, Conventional husbands and wives fear "losing themselves" to the marriage and employ such games as self-protective measures. What Conventional couples must learn as they mature is that a truly strong identity cannot be lost or stolen. Such fears tend to say more about the weakness of the individual than they do about the potentially "oppressive" nature of either a marriage partner or of the institution of marriage itself. Considering all these factors, Conventional marriages tend to be moderately stable and moderately satisfactory.

Now let's explore the two varieties of Conventional marriages: Storybook and Star marriages.

Storybook Marriages

MARITAL THEME: Finding their place in a world of conservative values.

This couples's search for their niche will eventually lead them to seek greater involvement in groups such as community organizations or religious institutions that are considered to reflect traditional values. The marriage itself has a traditional structure to it, however. Unlike the Shipwrecked Materialistic wife who had no choice but to stay home, the Conventional Storybook wife has other options available to her but chooses to stay home because she believes that role is important. Her employment before marriage was usually thought of as something to do until she achieved her primary goal of marriage and family. ("Someday my prince will come.") Though the Storybook wife may be publicly deferential to her husband, she definitely sees herself as the "woman behind the man" and will not hesitate to push him if she feels he is falling below his potential. The husband, for his part, is ambivalent about this pushing. On the one hand, he doesn't like to be told what to do. On the other hand, he doesn't mind being mothered.

The Conventional Storybook husband is the breadwinner of the family, but he tries to be careful not to lord his position over the family like a Shipwrecked Materialistic husband would. One major issue the Storybook husband deals with is that since he gets so much of his identity from being a (insert family name/cultural identity here) he may have a difficult time standing up to mummy and daddy, even when his marriage depends on it.

Spousal roles could best be defined as "semipermeable." The Storybook husband usually solicits his wife's opinions on the finances, but most of the time ends up explaining why his way is the best way to go. Likewise, the Storybook wife asks her husband's opinions on the managing of the domestic front, but then explains why her way is the best. In general, the spousal roles in Storybook marriages are more distinct and well defined than those of more satisfied couples further up the pathway. However, they are not nearly as rigid and legalistic as the roles in Shipwrecked marriages.

As I mentioned above, the primary danger to all Conventional marriages is "growing apart." For the Conventional Storybook marriage, this usually means that the husband throws himself into work, while the wife throws herself into maintaining the home and caring for the children. One day, the couple wakes up to find that they are living parallel lives. The only way to prevent this is for the husband and wife to at least maintain some interest in each other's worlds. This is difficult for some Conventional couples who can get a bit lazy about pushing themselves to share in activities with their mate that are not of great interest to themselves. Often what propels a couple through these selfish tendencies are the examples of other, more attentive married couples in the groups to which they belong. Conventional couples may be willing to ignore their own mate at times but they despise being found wanting by other members of their group. It is this accountability that—when it works well—reminds Conventional couples to care for their marriages. Those Conventional couples who belong to "values groups" that do not specifically support marriage run a considerably higher risk of divorce

Now let's look at the Storybook marriage's estranged cousin, the Star marriage.

Star Marriages

MARITAL THEME: Supporting and maintaining each other's place in the world.

The only real difference between Storybook and Star marriages is that Star couples build their marriages around more liberal political beliefs, including feminism. Likewise, rather than seeking more active involvement in traditional religious and community organizations as their Storybook cousins do, the Star couple often get involved in professional and political organizations and community groups with a more liberal social agenda.

The Star couple's marriage is the thing from which the husband and wife can draw strength to go out and conquer the world. Proving themselves in the workplace is perhaps the single most important agenda for the Star couple. Their work may or may not be glamorous, but this is less relevant than the fact that "doing the best job possible" or "shining" at the office is personally important. The Star couple is susceptible to all the pitfalls of their Storybook cousins. Only the details differ. For example, the Star couple's risk of growing apart is played out in both the husband and wife's devotion to their work. If the couple is not careful to share some interests and schedule some time to be together, their home can become the place where they carry on a collective monologue as they work on separate projects, coordinate separate schedules, and pursue separate civic involvements, but rarely, if ever, relate to one another.

Also, the Star couple, being consciously or unconsciously more sensitive to the motto, "the personal is political," is very attentive to domestic scorekeeping. Arguments about the "fair" division of labor are fairly common, especially in the earlier stages of the marriage. As for marital chicken, it is often played when negotiating work schedules. "You know I can't go to your office party on the third, I have a meeting that night. I would never ask you to give up an important meeting for me!" or "Of course I'd love to come home early and go to a movie but the project committee is meeting for dinner. You know how important this is to me. Why are you being so needy right when I'm getting my chance to shine?"

Children are also a sensitive issue for the Star couple, who tend to fear both "losing themselves" to the parenting role and what having children may do to the balance of power in the relationship. As with Storybook couples, Star couples need to remember that a truly solid identity cannot be lost. To achieve greater identity strength, Conventional couples will have to develop a clearer sense of their own values, ideals, and goals which will then form the basis of their marital imperative. This, more than anything, will move the marriage toward Exceptional couplehood (see below).

Recommendations for Conventional Couples

To move beyond the Conventional stage, couples must concentrate on the following.

1. *Solidify your value system.* The most important challenge that stands between the Conventional couple and Exceptional couplehood is developing a marital imperative: a deeply held and mutually shared set of values, ideals, and goals that will guide the couple's life and marriage. In order to become an Exceptional couple you must examine how your values can motivate you to give more of yourself than seems "fair" and make choices that might make you seem somewhat "unconventional" to others. For example, a more Conventional husband may excuse himself from acting lovingly toward his wife because he feels her present behavior does not warrant such generosity (and his friends may congratulate him for not being a doormat), but the Exceptional husband is more immune to such periodic lapses by his mate (after all, he has them too) and will continue to be loving even in the face of them because that is the kind of person he wishes to be when he "grows up." The Exceptional person will not allow himself to become a victim, but he also knows that to be true to himself, he must first be true to the values he upholds.

One major aid to the process of clarifying and solidifying one's values, ideals, and goals is pursuing a continually stronger identification with, and apprenticeship to, the specific ideals upheld by a particular values group (church or synagogue, men's and women's groups, political organizations). This is the method used by many "naturally occurring" Exceptional couples.

Up until now, the more Conventional couple has appreciated their particular values group for the comfort they receive, or sense of importance they derive, from being involved. For example, a Conventional couple might attend a particular church because, "even though we don't agree with many of the teachings, it gives us comfort to go," or they might belong to a civic organization because "it gives us a sense of purpose." This attitude is fine up to a point, but good as it is, it is basically a self-centered approach to faith and works. To move to the next level, couples must ask not what their values can do for them, but ask what they can do for their values, to borrow a phrase. Apprenticing themselves to a values group can provide the clarification, accountability, and support most people need to be true to their own values when the going gets tough. By way of example, some prominent couples who I believe (based on their writing and reputations) meet the criteria for at least the first category of Exceptional couplehood (the Partnership marriages) include movie critic Michael Medved and psychologist and author, Dr. Diane Medved; businessman and motivational speaker Stephen Covey and Sandra Covey; and nationally known child-care experts, Dr. William Sears and Martha Sears, R.N. In addition to the many admirable qualities about these couples, each is an active member of a strong faith community (Judaism, Mormonism, and Evangelical Protestantism, respectively.) Similarly, one can also have an Exceptional marriage based on more secular values. Perhaps a good example of this would be the marriage of Democratic political strategist James Carville and Republican political strategist Mary Matalin. From a psychological perspective, the "ism" you subscribe to is not as important as the need to become a hard-working, faithful apprentice of that "ism" in order to ultimately clarify your own beliefs and sense of self.

The idea of apprenticing oneself to a particular, organized values group is admittedly distasteful to the Western—and especially, American—mind. But Erik Erikson and Abraham Maslow's independent work on identity development, Lawrence Kohlberg's studies of moral development, and James Fowler's research on faith development all agree that often it is important for a value system to externally clarified before it can be adequately owned (internalized) by an individual. A person who would prefer to be his own moral compass (that is, who would attempt to develop a personal value system and marital imperative exclusive of a particular values group) would do well to remember that even the best compass needs a magnetic north against which to check itself. Faith communities and other values groups provide such a magnetic north.

All this aside, however you and your mate come to develop and practice your marital imperative, it will be your serious commitment to this shared mission statement that allows you to stop playing at both marital chicken and emotional or domestic scorekeeping, to no longer be loving only when your mate "deserves" such generosity, but also to be loving simply because that is the kind of person you wish to become when you grow up. This is often the single most difficult step for the Conventional couple to appreciate, but it is absolutely essential for Exceptional couplehood.

2. *Come out of your own world.* Even though Conventional marriages are founded on love, sometimes they can be a bit shallow with regard to intimacy especially considering the husband and wife's tendency to carve out their own worlds and then live in them exclusively. Storybook husbands may know little if anything about the running of their Storybook home. Storybook wives may not wish to be bored with the details of their husband's work. Star husbands and wives tend to be too wrapped up in their own work to take time to share their mate's world. In short, Conventional married couples are often too busy to relate to each other as much as they need to. This must stop if a Conventional couple intends to move into an Exceptional marriage. Couples must find ways to become both interested and active in each other's worlds. One well-known counselor asserts that a couple must spend at least fifteen hours per week working and talking together for their marriage to function well. How close do you come to this in your marriage?

3. *Refine your communication skills.* Even though Conventional couples are basically good at communicating their needs and emotions, there is always room for improvement. Conventional couples regularly experience communication breakdowns related to certain subtle but important stylistic differences. The chapters on Exceptional Rapport and Exceptional Negotiation will be especially helpful.

Having reviewed the most common marriages, let us move onto the two types of Exceptional marriages. As you read the following pages, you may be amazed by what a marital imperative empowers couples to become.

Exceptional Marriages

There are two major categories of Exceptional marriages. Each represents a different level of mastery of its marital imperative. The first type, accounting for the lion's share of exceptional couples, is the Partnership marriage, which is primarily concerned with pursuing and increasing personal competence. The first thing a marital imperative does for a person is make him or her aware of the areas of personal deficiency—whether due to a lack of interest or a lack of talent—and work to become more competent in those areas. The second type of Exceptional marriage is the Spiritual Peer marriage (a.k.a. the Romantic Peer marriage). Once the couple has achieved a higher level of competency they can begin to focus on pursuing both intimacy and actualization as a way of life. Let's briefly examine each of these.

Partnership Marriages

MARITAL THEME: The pursuit of competence and intimacy; the first fruits of a marital imperative.

After a couple clarifies their marital imperative, the first thing each spouse begins to do is ask, "What do I need to do in my marriage to be a better example of the positive characteristics and moral virtues (love, wisdom, integrity, creativity, etc.) that I hold dear?" The result of this first level of questioning is usually the person's decision to pursue competence in areas he or she was previously uninterested or un-talented in. A husband may no longer wait to be asked by his wife to "help" around the house; instead he intentionally works to become more aware of the things that need to be done and does them. A wife may begin to ask herself what jobs or responsibilities she pushes off onto her husband simply because she doesn't enjoy them, and then works to develop greater competence in these areas. (See chapter 6.)

In true Partnership marriages, no job is off-limits for either husband or wife. Both work to be equally aware of all the domestic, romantic, and financial responsibilities of marriage. Both expect themselves to do a job if they happen to trip over it first or are more available to do it, even if it is not traditionally their area of expertise.

This pursuit of competence allows the Partnership couple to achieve three things: the victory of egalitarianism over mere equality, the removal of self-protective barriers to intimacy, and Exceptional Rapport and Negotiation.

1. *Egalitarianism over equality.* In her book, *Peer Marriage,* Dr. Pepper Schwartz noted that one factor which separated Exceptional (or as she called them "peer couples") from Conventional couples was the preference of egalitarianism over mere equality. Basically, this is the difference between marriage as a "50/50 proposition" and marriage as a "100/100 partnership." Conventional couples make a huge issue out of dividing up chores or spheres of influence into nice equal piles to safeguard both "fairness" and the "balance of power." By contrast, Partnership couples don't have the same need to divide

everything up into equal piles to prove they are equal. Partnership husbands and wives know that they are equal without the aid of such games. They expect themselves and their partners to give 100 percent at all times, or at least as much as is humanly possible. No particular responsibility is beneath either one of them. This leads to what I call a dance of competence—the gracefully efficient and often selfless manner in which Partners accomplish the tasks of daily living.

The essence of marital egalitarianism is an equality of *being,* not just an equality of chores. This is an essential ingredient in the deepest form of intimacy, which Partners are on their way to attaining.

2. *True intimacy.* Being safe in the knowledge that no matter how much you give to a marriage you will not be taken for granted is a very freeing experience. This freedom allows couples to start letting down the barriers and stop playing games with each other. Now the two merely semipermeable worlds of the Conventional couple begin to come together as never before. Husband and wife are both beginning to become more interested and more competent in each other's domains. As a result, everything they share, every chore of married life, presents one more opportunity to draw closer together, to become more intimate.

Likewise, having made a commitment to their marital imperative, the Partnership husband and wife are beginning to see each other as their best hope for becoming the people they want to be by the end of their lives. I will explain this process in greater detail in the chapter on designing your own marital imperative. For now, suffice it to say that as the Partnership couple moves through this stage, they become more and more convinced that the most important work of marriage is helping each other grow in identity strength and move toward the actualization of their shared spiritual values, moral ideals, and emotional goals. To this end, the Partnership couple, indeed all the Exceptional couples, consider themselves uniquely qualified to help each other fulfill their life's mission and value system. This attitude lends itself to the extraordinary intimacy, gratitude, satisfaction, and longevity Exceptional couples enjoy. A husband and wife may meet more attractive, wealthier, or better socially positioned people along the way, but they are convinced that no one is better equipped than their mate to help them achieve actualization.

3. *Exceptional rapport and negotiation.* Chapters 7 and 8 will examine these qualities in detail. The intense interest in and sharing of each other's worlds tends to remove the last major barriers to communication. The discussions that result from working side by side in almost every area of life lead to a deep level of rapport and understanding. Besides this, Exceptional couples are able to exhibit a high degree of respect for one another even when they disagree, and arguments, for the most part, are experienced as "deep muscle massages," which may feel uncomfortable at the time but will afterward leave the marriage more relaxed and flexible.

Partnership marriages come in two varieties: Traditional and Modern. Traditional partners build their marriage around more conservative or religious values. The husband is usually the breadwinner, but he is expected—and expects himself—to be every bit as competent a parent and homemaker as his wife. He is attentive and intimately involved in the home life and domestic work. Likewise he and his wife are emotional and communicative peers. They both work hard to communicate their emotions well and their needs respectfully.

For her part, the Traditional Partnership wife is an active participant in financial planning. She feels it is very important to contribute to the family finances. Even if she is not employed out of the home, she may do things like homeschool the children or make other significant contributions of service and skills that give her family an economic edge. This stay-at-home mom is not likely to be found among the "ladies who lunch."

Conventional stay-at-home moms tend to be torn. On the one hand, they feel that what they do is valuable; on the other hand, they struggle with society's (and sometimes even their husband's) general dismissiveness of women who work at home. Often they feel inferior to their Star wife friends. Traditional Partnership wives experience no such identity crisis. They are sure of the importance and financial value of their contribution to the family. And they find deep fulfillment in the hard work they do.

Like all couples in the Exceptional category, Traditional Partnership couples work to cultivate similar interests. Most times they would rather do something they don't enjoy as long as they are doing it with their mate rather than do something they do enjoy with someone else. It is extremely rare for the Partnership spouse to say, "You know I hate doing such and such. Call one of your buddies/girlfriends." But make no mistake: even though the Partnership couple is usually together, a Partnership husband or wife is always free to go out with his or her own friends. Personal boundaries and the need to be alone are respected. (Shipwrecked spouses, on the other hand, are always together because it is too much of a hassle to get permission from their mate to go out alone.)

Modern Partnerships, the second type of Partnership marriage, are built around more secular and liberal ideals, but the dynamics of the relationship are basically the same as their Traditional counterparts. They value egalitarianism, work to share in each other's worlds, and they do not keep score over who does what because they are confident that each is doing as much as possible at all times. As far as marital structure goes, the only real difference between Traditional and Modern Partners is what they consider to be a more efficient use of resources. Where Traditional Partners' values suggest that it is preferable to have one person more or less oversee the domestic responsibilities and one person more or less oversee the financial affairs, the Modern Partners' values dictate that both the husband and wife should contribute as much as possible to every sphere with no one (at least in theory) exerting too much influence over any one area. On the downside, this tends to make Modern Partners slightly more harried than their Traditional counterparts. On the upside, this tends to eliminate the temptation to coast that sometimes affects Traditional Partners. Take your pick. Both marriages are fantastic, and people should consider themselves blessed to be in either version of Partnership marriage.

Recommendations for Partnership Couples

No doubt some of you are wondering what could possibly come after this. It is true, Partnership marriages are wonderful but there is one more step to take if a couple is so inclined (the Spiritual Peer marriage). To do this, the Partnership couple must work to accomplish two things:

1. *Develop a truly spiritual sexuality.* Strangely enough, the deep friendship and intimacy which Partnership couples share can, in some cases, put a temporary damper on the sexual relationship. How can this be? For all our claims that we are a sexually liberated lot, most

people still speak of sex using derogatory terms. We refer to sex as "being naughty" or "getting nasty," and we often use sex as a way to prove ourselves, or rebel against authority, or get in touch with our "wild" or "bad" side.

But in a Partnership marriage there is little that is negative, there is nothing to prove, and there is no authority to rebel against. As such, the negative concepts which define so many people's sexuality no longer apply. As one Partnership wife said, "It's hard for me to 'get nasty' with somebody I love and respect so much." In her book, *Peer Marriage,* Dr. Schwartz refers to this phenomenon as an "incest taboo." (The idea that two people can be so close and respect each other so much that sex no longer seems an appropriate way to relate.)

To overcome this problem, the couple must mine the spiritual core of their sexuality. This involves challenging the basic foundations of contemporary sexual attitudes and discovering how married sexuality is not only a celebration of goodness, but also an opportunity for actualization. Chapter 10 will deal with this issue further.

2. *Exhibit a willingness to make financial sacrifices.* The Partnership couple is already risking their basic acceptance by pursuing their value of intimacy and togetherness despite the disapproving comments of those more Conventional friends who keep saying "you need to take time for *yourself.* Don't forget about *yourself.*" Now, to move to the next level, most Partnership couples are going to have to deemphasize the importance of financial success. This is not to say that one must embrace poverty, simply that one must be willing to set serious limits on anything that distracts one from actualizing his or her value system. For most people, pursuing material success is a pretty big distraction. Those Partnership couples who are willing to scale back on their income, or at least decrease the energy they expend pursuing career success, have the best chance of achieving not only the highest known form of marriage, but also the strongest known level of identity strength.

Spiritual Peer Marriages

MARITAL THEME: The pursuit of intimacy, simplification, and actualization.

As far as current research goes, this is the top of the marital food chain. If both types of Exceptional couples (the Partnership marriages and Spiritual Peer marriages) were combined, they would total about 15 percent of all marriages (and 7 percent of first marriages). Spiritual Peers alone probably account for no more than 4 percent of *all* marriages.

Spiritual Peers focus on intimacy in the context of self-actualization. You will recall that to be "actualized" is to be a person who is a joyful, living, breathing example of a particular value system. For the Spiritual Peer couple, nothing is more important than helping each other live out a deeply held set of spiritual values, moral ideals, and emotional goals. While Partnership couples still struggle with how to apply their deeply held ideals in their unique circumstances, often seeking clarifying advice from an important involvement in a values group, Spiritual Peers have almost completely internalized—or "own"—their values. For the most part, they have incorporated the tenets of their values group into their lives and no longer have to check with anyone else to see if they are "doing it right" (though they are still open to criticism from credible sources and actively seek opportunities for continued growth).

Three qualities are the hallmarks of these marriages: simplification, competence, and egalitarianism. We have discussed two of the three in relation to Partnership marriages, but each is exhibited in a purer form in Spiritual Peer marriages. First, simplification: Both husband and wife are definitely off the fast track. They *could* work more, but they have come to the conclusion that the time and money isn't worth the cost to their pursuit of intimacy and other values. Spiritual Peers aren't deadbeats, they just have more important things to do. In particular, loving each other and their children. Spiritual Peers are not martyrs. They don't give up anything they really need, but they know how to give up everything that is not valuable, like approval or more money than their needs and most important wants require.

Second, both husband and wife are competent at all aspects of family life. At this level, the dance of competence, which began around household responsibilities now extends to every other relationship task. Who works outside the home? Whoever feels their values calling them to do so at this time. Who takes care of the kids? They both do. Spiritual Peers are co-parents in the extreme. Who plans the social calendar and "couple time"? Both husband and wife are equally aware and skilled at handling their relationship and social calendars.

Third, they value egalitarianism over equality. Again, Spiritual Peers represent the refinement of this quality which was first witnessed in the Partnership marriage. You will recall that people who value egalitarianism *know* they are equal and don't feel the need to prove it by dividing jobs up into nice even piles or by declaring certain tasks to be beneath them. As good as Partnership couples are at this, sometimes they still struggle with scorekeeping (albeit to a significantly lesser degree than Conventional couples). By contrast, Spiritual Peers are old hands at egalitarianism and the dance of competence. Through the years, both husband and wife have demonstrated their desire to never take each other for granted, and so scorekeeping and marital chicken are distant memories.

A silly example might help clarify how a couple going up the Relationship Pathway grows in competence and egalitarianism. The Shipwrecked wife might rather die a slow, torturous death than change a lightbulb if she considered it her husband's job, but she would exhaust three hundred times as much energy nagging him to do it. The Conventional wife would change the bulb, if her husband didn't get to it when she asked, but she would secretly resent his dereliction of duty for the rest of her life, or at least for the rest of the day. The Partnership wife changes the bulb without a second thought. The Peer wife would not only change the bulb without thinking about it, but also might have the whole house rewired—to code—by the time her husband came home.

Likewise, the Shipwrecked husband would consider watching his children "baby-sitting." He is loath to do it and looks for the earliest opportunity to sack out on the sofa. The Conventional husband knows that he should want to watch his kids, but it would only be a matter of time before he got bored and sent them to play in the basement so he could get some work done. The Partnership husband would eagerly play with the children and would be happy to give his wife a break whenever she asked for it. And the Peer husband would be begging his wife to go out so that he could get some alone time with his kids (and the house would be immaculate when she got back).

This couple is so good at taking care of themselves and each other that to outsiders their marriage just seems to happen magically. They are the highest functioning examples of what Dr. Don Jackson and William Lederer of the Palo Alto Mental Research Center described as "collaborative geniuses." Of course, a great deal of very hard work goes into making these marriages work, but it is most definitely a labor of love. Spiritual Peers are each other's best friends, have virtually no secrets from each other, and have achieved a level of spiritual sexuality that is truly enviable. Unlike couples in less-good marriages who go through periods of boredom with each other, the Spiritual Peers' relationship actually becomes more vital, exciting, fun, and fulfilling as the years go by.

If they struggle with anything, it is their relative social isolation. Spiritual Peers are too busy loving each other and living their own lives to have the energy for the *Sturm und Drang* that comes with having too many acquaintances. This is in contrast to Shipwrecked couples, who avoid others because they fear them, and Apprenticeship couples, who gorge themselves on a frenzy of casual acquaintances and social commitments.

Abraham Maslow, developer of the Hierarchy of Needs, researched self-actualizing people and his findings apply to all the Exceptional couples, especially to Spiritual Peers. They are accepting of themselves and others, are at peace when life becomes unpredictable, are spontaneous and creative, have a good sense of humor, value their privacy, can take care of themselves, are capable of deeply intimate relationships, and have an open, positive attitude about life. They are the couples—indeed, the people—we all want to be when we grow up.

Can Your Marriage Be Exceptional?

After reading about Exceptional couples it would be possible to despair of ever achieving such a lofty status, but be encouraged. This book is mostly concerned with helping you find your way into the first of the Exceptional marriages (the Traditional and Modern Partnerships). From that point, every couple must find their own way to actualization and Spiritual Peerdom. Likewise, it is important to note that the majority of Exceptional Partnership couples started out in more Conventional relationships. Only after developing their marital imperative and clinging to it through the storms of life did they find themselves—often unexpectedly so—at a more gratifying level of marital intimacy.

A perfect example of this growth through struggle would be Kenny and Bobbi McCaughey. They began life together as an average working-class couple with a strong connection to their community and church. Eventually they became parents of their daughter Mikayla and the famous McCaughey septuplets.

In one book, *Seven From Heaven,* Kenny McCaughey describes his dramatic walk down the road toward what I would call Exceptional husbandhood through the pregnancy and subsequent birth of the couple's septuplets. While his wife was confined to extreme bedrest from the earliest weeks of gestation, McCaughey found himself challenging all the comfortable rules of Conventional married life. He was forced to challenge his competencies more quickly and more pervasively than you or I will probably ever have to, and through his labor he developed what I would consider to be Exceptional gratitude toward his wife, whom he reports he always loved dearly, but without really appreciating the full value of her gift to the marriage until their blessed crisis compelled him to walk in her shoes for an extended period. Through that tumultuous pregnancy and the chaotic months following the septuplets' birth, the only thing the McCaugheys had to hold on to was what I would call their marital imperative, the theme of their marriage, summed up by a line in song they sang to each other at their wedding: "And the world shall know that we are a household of faith." As the world today can attest, they are.

Not knowing the McCaugheys personally (and considering that their book was mostly about their children and not their marriage), I cannot say if they would consider themselves to be an Exceptional couple as of this writing, but I can say with confidence that they are traveling down that road, and if they continue to cling to their marital imperative as a way of life, they will surely reach their destination.

And so will you, because as difficult as the journey to Exceptional couplehood is, it is also the journey for which each and every one of us was made. Every particle of every human being—body and soul— cries out to made whole by love: by being loved by others, by loving others, and by love itself. What better opportunity to pursue this most natural of callings than the opportunity presented by your marriage, which is nothing if it is not a "school of love" in every sense of that phrase.

The remaining chapters of this book will help you discover the skills and resources you will need to complete your journey up the Relationship Pathway toward Exceptional couplehood. I invite you and your beloved to begin your adventure with the next chapter by developing a vital, compelling, and challenging marital imperative.

3

Designing a Marital Imperative

Marriage... transforms a human action into an instrument of the divine action.

—JACQUES LECLERCQ

MAX AND SHELBY have been married for sixteen years. The thing that Shelby says she likes most about Max is his ability to "keep her focused."

"When I was in college, I was struggling to figure out what I wanted to do when I got out. Around that time I took a philosophy class that changed my life. The professor tried to make the subject more relevant by asking us to focus on not just what kind of work we wanted to do but what kind of people we wanted to be. He asked us to consider our assigned readings from the perspective of finding some guiding principles—a 'worldview' he called it. This way, regardless of what we decided to do with our lives we could define success by how we conducted ourselves. I guess I kind of ran with that assignment. I came up with a list of qualities that were important to me, things that I knew would keep me centered regardless of how much or how little money I made or where I ended up in life. I decided to gauge my definition of success by how well I was living up to my principles, and rather than letting these be pie-in-the-sky ideals, I really tried to keep them in mind as I went through my day. I even weeded out potential boyfriends based on whether or not they brought out more of those particular qualities in me. I wanted a marriage partner who was going to help keep me focused on what was really important.

"A lot of times, guys would look at me like I had two heads when I would talk about this stuff. They accused me of 'thinking too much' and told me there'd be plenty of time to worry about all that later on, and I should just relax. My friends kept telling me that my standards were too unrealistic. I was beginning to think that I would have to choose between my value system and getting a steady boyfriend. I know that sounds hopelessly shallow of me, but what can I say? It's how I felt. Thankfully I didn't have to chuck everything because soon afterward I met Max, and he understood me perfectly."

Max picked up the story at this point. "My mom died when I was young and I think that clarified what was really important to me. Mom had this Hummel figurine collection. She used to love those things. She spent hours pouring over catalogs, going to collector's shows—whatever. Anyway, after she died my dad sold them all. He said it was just too sad to have them around the house. Obviously the whole thing was very traumatic for me, but oddly enough, Dad selling her stuff bothered me in some ways even more than her dying. For the life of me, I couldn't figure out why. It took me a long time, but I finally realized that her whole life was represented by those figurines, and I started thinking, 'You know what? Her whole life was just packed up in a box and sold.' Then I started thinking about my own life. When it was all over, would it be packed into a box and be sold too? I guess the whole experience made me kind of morbid as a teenager, but when I came through the depression part of it, I realized that there was no way I wanted my life to be like that. I started thinking about what kind of person I wanted to be, what kind of contribution I wanted to make, and I read a lot about relationships. With my mom gone, and my dad throwing himself into work so he wouldn't have time to think too much, I realized how irreplaceable relationships were, and I wanted to make sure I would know how to get the most out of my future family life.

"I was about twenty when I met Shelby, and I think I knew the first night we went out that she was the one for me. She was telling me about what she stood for and how anybody that she ended up with had to make it easier to stand for those things and I was just blown away.

I thought to myself, 'This is exactly the person I need in my life.'"

Shelby continued, "We've really helped each other stay true to our ideals throughout our marriage. A lot of the time it was very difficult, but I'm glad we did it because I think we've helped each other become better people. I know I wouldn't like the person I am today half as much if it weren't for Max constantly bringing my words back to me and encouraging me to keep those promises I made to myself back in college, to live out those ideals whether I felt like it or not. And I try to do the same for him."

Max interrupted. "We keep each other honest. And we love each other more because of it."

The Marital Imperative: Five Benefits

As you saw in the last chapter, building your life and relationship around a marital imperative—a deeply held, mutually shared set of spiritual values, moral ideals, and emotional goals—yields several benefits. In this chapter, you will examine some of these advantages more closely. Likewise, you and your mate will be given an opportunity to design your own marital imperative, empowering you to enjoy:

1. Greater identity strength and marital satisfaction.
2. More peace in uncertain times.
3. Greater personal competence and self-confidence.
4. Deeper marital intimacy.
5. Greater expectations for marital longevity.

Of course, a marital imperative is the key which unlocks all the other Exceptional Couple qualities outlined in this book: fidelity, love, service, rapport, negotiation, gratitude, joy, and a spiritual sexuality. While you will have a chance to learn more about these qualities later, I invite you to take a moment to examine the five direct benefits of a marital imperative.

The First Benefit: Greater Identity Strength and Marital Satisfaction

If you've ever watched a daytime talk show, you've probably heard that it's important to have an identity before you get into a serious relationship.

While most people have heard this, few really understand what it means. The reason identity is so important to marital success is because it alone determines your marital theme (recall the Relationship Pathway). To truly appreciate the influence identity strength wields upon your marital theme we need to briefly examine a few questions: What, exactly, is an "identity"? How do you know if you have one? How do you know how strong it is? And what does any of this have to do with the success and happiness of your marriage?

What is identity? Simply put, your identity is the theme around which you build your life. Everyone likes to think they have a strong sense of self, but as you saw in the last chapter, some themes are better than others. For example, escape, basic needs, work, social roles, and possessions are all too transient to qualify as good identity-making material. People who have the most identity strength are those who are primarily concerned with developing positive character traits, pursuing spiritual growth, and exhibiting moral courage. How much of an identity you have is directly dependent upon your ability to identify the qualities you wish to exhibit, the ideals you wish to be known for, and the one or two accomplishments that you absolutely must achieve between today and the day you die.

A good assessment of a healthy identity is what I call the "bad country song" test. It goes like this (feel free to hum along):

> If ya lost yer friends, and ya lost yer job
> and got throwed out of yer house.
> If yer dog ran away and yer truck got stoled
> and yer preacher ran away with yer spouse,
> If they let ya down and you felt just as low
> as a hoss gettin' kicked with a spur.
> Let me ask ya just one question pardner,
> Would ya still know who ya were?

Kind of makes you want to cry, doesn't it?

As silly as that song is, every one of those things has happened to somebody at some time. They could happen to you. Throughout the trials of life, it is absolutely essential to remember that, at its core, a solid identity does not depend as much upon work, roles, or possessions as it does upon a deeply internalized set of values, ideals, and goals which must guide and clarify every action and decision of your life.

How can you tell how strong your identity is? You know the strength of your identity by how much the values, ideals, and goals I referred to above are actually represented in your everyday life and choices. Answer the following question:

> Could a complete stranger look at the way you live, the choices you make, and the things you give your time and energy to, and know—without your having to say a word—what spiritual values, moral ideals, and emotional goals you believe are most important to you?

> ___ Absolutely   ___ Sort of   ___ Not on your life

The degree to which others can accurately determine what you claim to stand for by examining the choices you make, the manner in which you apportion your time, and the way you sacrifice certain things so that you can do other things is perhaps the best measurement of your identity strength.

Now, everyone believes in the importance of values, ideals, and goals, at least superficially. The problem is that many people excuse themselves from living out these principles because they believe they suffer from extenuating circumstances. The woman in an unhappy marriage believes herself to be a loving person and yet refuses to act in a loving way toward her husband because "he doesn't deserve it." A husband believes himself to be generous and giving, but is neglectful of his wife because "she knows I love her. Besides, marriages are either good or they aren't. You shouldn't have to work so hard all the time." Parents say their children are their most important priority and then spend an average of fifteen minutes a day with their kids because their lives are chock-full of so many other "less important" things. Granted, we all fall short sometimes. But it is one thing to fall short, accept responsibility for it, and work toward making the necessary changes, and it is another thing to make excuses. People with strong identities don't make excuses, not even good ones, for failing to fulfill their obligation to live out their own value systems.

Another common error people make is assuming they have a strong identity because they scream a lot. They equate making noise with standing up for what they believe in. Case in point: One client told me that she was a strong person because she always verbally challenged her husband for taking her for granted. The problem was that she never made good on any of her threats. All she did was scream. When I challenged her appalling lack of follow-through, she would only say, "Why should I inconvenience myself? He's the one with the problem."

This woman insisted she was standing up for herself, but she was shooting herself in the foot. The point is, people with true identity strength don't just make noise, they also set limits (based upon their principles) and follow through with those limits.

When it comes to identity strength, congruence is key. If you have a strong identity, then you exhibit remarkable congruence between what you claim to stand for and how you live.

What's this all got to do with relationships? The first thing a solid identity does for a marriage is to take what begins as an institution for convenience and companionship, and empower it to become an instrument for your actualization. In other words, when you build your life around a lesser theme, such as meeting basic needs, finding companionship, work, you have a tendency to think of marriage as a "nice thing to have," like a comfy chair or a guaranteed date for bowling night. And, of course, when the chair is no longer comfy or you sour on bowling, then it makes a great deal of sense to simply move on to the next "nice thing."

By contrast, when your life and relationship revolves around a compelling set of spiritual values, moral ideals, and emotional goals, then every interaction—pleasant or unpleasant—between you and your mate becomes another opportunity to pursue those very principles and qualities you hold most dear. For example, when you are stressed, do you lash out at your mate or do you look for ways to work with him or her and find answers? When you are irritated with your partner, do you say whatever cruel thing comes into your mind or do you seek greater understanding? When there is tension in your marriage, do you refuse to be loving toward your mate because he or he doesn't deserve such generosity or do you choose to be loving because exhibiting love is important to you? We all know the choices we are *supposed* to make, but the only way we will be able to motivate ourselves to cheerfully make those choices is if we have a solid commitment to our principles. Otherwise, it is just too easy to find reasonable excuses which will let us off the hook.

When a couple builds their life and relationship around one of the lesser themes, it really doesn't matter to them if they have a great marriage or not because, regardless, they draw comfort from the things that *are* most important: their escapes, possessions, work, community involvements, other friends. But if you build your life and relationship around a marital imperative, your deeply held, mutually shared set of values, ideals, and goals—then what matters most to you is having a great marriage because having a great marriage gives you an opportunity like no other to practice generosity, love, understanding—all the qualities that your happiness and your fulfillment require you to pursue between now and the end of your life.

This makes all the difference in a marriage. Most people are willing to change things about themselves if the change isn't too difficult and the ongoing marital peace depends upon it. But what if, for some reason, you need to challenge yourself in a way that makes you truly uncomfortable, and, moreover, things are not peaceful between you and your mate? Then what will motivate you to make the changes necessary to put your relationship back on track? If you build your identity and relationship around one of the lesser themes, then the answer is "nothing," but if you build your life and marriage around actualizing a specific set of deeply held values, ideals, and goals, then your motivation will be greater faithfulness to your own identity and marital imperative. Let me give you an example.

Janice and Bill came to me for marriage counseling. At the outset, they were locked in a deadly game of marital chicken and neither one intended to blink first. Bill needed to set some boundaries with his mother, who tended to make unreasonable demands and often cut in on his time with his wife and children. Janice needed to become more comfortable demonstrating her affection for Bill. Each felt that the other's deportment provided a poor motivation to change their own behavior.

The first thing I did was to separate Bill and Janice and ask them who they wanted to be when they "grew up," that is, what qualities did they want to be known for at the end of their lives. Having compiled a list of qualities like "loving, strong, independent, peaceful, generous, creative," I then asked Janice and Bill what they would need to change about their own behavior in their marriage in order to be more faithful examples of these qualities.

Shortly after this exercise, they began to see how playing marital chicken to "get at" each other was rather like slapping themselves in the face to spite their mate. In other words, Janice and Bill began to see that, even more important than the fact that they were letting each other down, they were not being true to themselves when they behaved as they had been. Bill realized that to be faithful to his ideal of being "independent and strong" he had to set limits with his mother—not because Janice told him to, but *for his own sake*. Janice was able to see that if she really wished to be a "loving person" at the end of her life, then she had better start increasing her capacity for affection today. Not because Bill wanted her to do it, but because "being loving" was important to her own self-concept. Within a matter of weeks, both Janice and Bill were freely and willingly enacting the changes they had previously only argued about for months. As they solidified their principles into a marital imperative they also began to learn how to avoid future bouts of marital chicken, and they discovered how to respectfully keep each other on task through the normal ups and downs of married life.

Janice and Bill are good examples of this second way identity strength affects marital satisfaction: by allowing you to stop playing games with each other so you can become the people you need to be, in order to have the marriage you want to have.

The Second Benefit: Peace in Uncertain Times

The second gift a marital imperative brings to both a husband and wife is a sense of peace in times of uncertainty. When you build your marriage around one of the lesser themes, and your world begins to fall apart, there is nothing to hold on to. Threats to your ability to meet your needs, pay your bills, or keep your personally meaningful job and social roles are no longer simply serious problems, they become identity problems.

But when you build your life around a marital imperative, even when your world is in crisis you can still cling to the values, ideals, and goals which form the core of your identity. When the McCaugheys were preparing for the arrival of their septuplets, they were moving into uncharted territory. No one they knew could tell them how to proceed; nothing in their lives had prepared them for what was to come. As Kenny McCaughey put it, "This was not a Kenny-sized problem." The only thing that saw them through was clinging like mad to their marital imperative, "we are a household of faith."

When my wife and I lost our first child through miscarriage, no one knew what to say. We didn't know how to recover, and we didn't know how to make sense out of our loss—or even if sense could be made of it. Only by holding fast to our own marital imperative of pursuing love, seeking wisdom, and listening for God did we come to see that tragedy as the catalyst which enabled us to become the very different couple, and eventually parents, we are today.

One family I know barely escaped with their lives when a tornado destroyed their home. The process of rebuilding was difficult, especially since the insurance was slow to pay and they had no relatives in the area. But by holding fast to their marital imperative— "pursuing strength, love, and togetherness no matter where life takes us"—they were able to keep from turning on each other in anger and work toward reclaiming their lives from the ruin and building a new home for their family.

When a couple builds their life and marriage around one of the lesser marital themes—work, for example—then when that work ends, the couple looks out and sees nothing but blackness, doubt, and depression. Alternatively, when a couple who builds their lives around a marital imperative loses an important job or role, they draw real comfort from their ability to continue being a couple that lives to exhibit love, generosity, service, and wisdom in all areas of their life until a new job or role presents itself.

There is an old Quaker hymn that goes, "No storm can shake my inmost calm, while to that rock I'm clinging." Psychologically speaking, a marital imperative is "the rock" of one's marriage. And no storm can shake the calm you find in your soul and relationship while you are standing high upon it.

The Third Benefit: Greater Competence and Self-Confidence

Margaret and Forest were constantly battling over their division of household labor. Both worked out of the home and both felt they did more than their "fair share" around the house. The fighting had gotten so bad that when one of them did perform some service, the other could not feel any gratitude. He or she could only respond with some version of, "It's about time you're doing something around here."

I had them complete the "who do you want to be when you grow up" exercise. After they had given me their lists, I suggested one addition. I asked them both if they would like to be known as "competent people." Both Margaret and Forest had a strong, positive response to this quality. I then asked them which response was more consistent with their vision of a "competent person": sitting around whining and arguing about how much he or she has to do, or identifying and completing a task when he or she happens upon it? They immediately saw my point, but Margaret raised an excellent objection. She said, "Yes, but what if I did that and Forest just hung back and let me handle everything?" Forest, of course, responded with a similar jab, at which point I said to both of them, "Look, neither of you wants to allow your marriage to turn you into a couple of incompetent, bickering whiners. I want you both to make a commitment to yourselves to pursue competence in your home—for your own sake, not your mate's—for the next three months. If, after that time, either of you discover that you are married to a user, then you have my permission to divorce, but until that time, as far as I am concerned, what you have is a case of the pot calling the kettle black." They accepted my challenge. We established a few additional ground rules in that session and I spent the next few weeks weaning them from their pathological addictions to domestic scorekeeping.

Within four weeks they were a different couple. Not only was their home running more smoothly and the gratitude coming back into their marriage, but the couple's sense of satisfaction with themselves was on the rise as well. As Forest put it, "At the beginning it took a real effort to do things around the house and not resent Margaret. But after a while, I started realizing that I felt good about myself when I stayed on top of things. I even refinished our dining room chairs. I never did anything like that before." Margaret added, "And I think that with both of us working to improve our competencies around the home at the same time, we kind of fed off each other. You know, we're both a little competitive." She laughed dryly. "You probably hadn't noticed that before, right?"

A marital imperative reminds a couple of their responsibility to themselves to pursue competence and to actualize their personal mission statements. After all, this is the one thing upon which a positive self-concept hangs, being true to one's ideals. Working together on a clearly identified set of values, goals, and ideals (a marital imperative) increases the chances that both the husband and the wife will become the people they want to be by the end of their lives, leading to what Erikson called "ego-integrity," a deep sense of rightness about one's self and one's life.

The Fourth Benefit: Greater Intimacy

The first way a marital imperative builds intimacy is by challenging a husband and wife to become more competent in areas they formerly left to their mate to handle. Recall what you learned about Partnership marriages. As the couple becomes more interested and competent in each other's worlds, they have more to talk about and more to share and, therefore, they have more intimacy.

The second way a marital imperative builds intimacy is by helping a couple truly appreciate that they are each other's unique and best hope for becoming the people they want to be at the end of their lives. Marriage, more than any other type of relationship, work, role, or social outlet, challenges a person to actualize the values and ideals he or she holds most dear. Some of you may doubt this. Let me challenge you a bit.

Have you ever noticed that it is sometimes easier to be nice to other people's children and other people's husbands and wives than it is to be kind to your own? Have you ever noticed how it can be relatively easy to be a thoughtful, generous person at the office, but how difficult it sometimes is to be the same way at home? Why is that?

We all have our public faces, and somehow, it is easier to be the people we want others to think we are when we wear those faces. But when we come home, we become who we really are—who we are when we don't have anyone to impress; who we are when we are at our most vulnerable, and supposedly, most intimate. When you see yourself reflected in the eyes of your mate, you see most clearly how near or far you actually come to fulfilling the values, ideals, and goals you hold closest to your heart. As Tom Monaghan, founder of Domino's Pizza and a prominent philanthropist, joked in a recent interview, "The pope says, 'Good man, good man!' but my wife says, 'That doesn't cut any ice with me!' Her role is to keep me in my place."

That is exactly what every husband and wife is supposed to do for each other. Show us who we *really* are, and help us become who we someday hope to be. You can fool your coworkers, you can fool your friends, you might even be able to fool the pope, but your wife and your kids have got you pegged. You can either run from the challenge this presents (which is what many Shipwrecked and Conventional couples do) or you can embrace it and, with the help of your marriage, become even better than the person you only pretend to be in public. A marital imperative makes this cooperative, intimate effort possible.

The final way a marital imperative enhances intimacy is that it makes one appreciate one's mate for both his or her strengths and weaknesses. Other people may have strengths similar to your mate's, but no one can offer the unique combination of strengths and weaknesses your mate brings to your relationship. Together, they present a tailormade opportunity to challenge your own deficiencies.

While it might be easy to see how a couple could make use of each other's strengths to grow, how is it possible to use each other's faults? Most of the time when you encounter a weakness in your mate, you have one of two reactions. The first is to ignore it. Yes, it's there. Yes, it's irritating. But, "what are you going to do?" The second reaction is to humiliate your mate for the shortcoming. "I can't believe you." "Why do you always have to do that?" "Sometimes you can be such a jerk."

When we choose either of these responses, we are missing out on an opportunity to pursue our own growth as well as an opportunity to grow in patience. In an encounter group I attended, the group leaders challenged any attendee who complained about his or her mate, children, boss, or anyone else and posed the question, "What does that say about you?" (The father of Gestalt therapy, Fritz Perls, used to make extensive use of this very effective technique, called "playing the projection" in his own therapeutic system.) After the complainers got over the initial shock and irritation provoked by such a comment, they began to see that every weakness in someone else pointed to something the complainers could change about themselves in order to grow and potentially improve their circumstances. Thus, the woman who complained about her "rotten kids" realized that she needed to become a more consistent disciplinarian; the husband who complained about his wife's insensitivity realized that his own perfectionism often drove her to ignore him; the wife who was upset by her husband's inattention realized that, other than nagging him, she had not done anything in recent memory to make herself worth paying attention to.

Granted, these insights didn't immediately change the children's rottenness, the wife's insensitivity, or the husband's inattention, but they had several other benefits. First, they stopped the "plaintiffs" from getting choked on their own self-righteousness. Second, they helped them see that they were not helpless bystanders—that they could do something either to effect change, or at least to become stronger people in their own right. Finally, they helped them exhibit more patience when dealing with others' faults.

While a marital imperative will probably never enable us to rejoice over our mate's weaknesses, it will show us how to make use of them. So, even while your mate is addressing his or her shortcomings, you can be patient, and maybe even grateful to your mate for allowing you to walk alongside and address your own.

The Fifth Benefit: Greater Expectations for Marital Longevity

Perhaps the major reason a marital imperative is superior to the other marital themes is its ability to lend lifelong relevance to a marriage. Most of the lesser marital themes are especially vulnerable to obsolescence. For example, if a couple builds their marriage around the theme of financial security, chances are their marriage may suffer a serious threat if the couple encounters hard times or the husband or wife meets a person who offers greater financial promise. Likewise, if a couple builds their marriage around the theme of companionship, they may suffer a serious crisis when the husband or wife meets a more interesting, attractive, or sympathetic companion. What makes some goals more compelling than others (and, in turn, some marriages better than others) is the level of difficulty involved in achieving a marital goal, because once a couple fulfills their marital theme (that is, achieves their ultimate goal) the marriage enters a crisis phase during which the couple stands around looking blankly at each other muttering "Now what?" as they try to think up new reasons to justify the continued existence of their relationship. In our disposable culture, when marriages encounter such a crisis of relevance, many couples simply discard their relationship and start again. While these husbands or wives may not like to put it so coldly, it would be true to say that their present partner has outlived his or her usefulness. And so, rather than seeking to work with their present partner to create a new, superior marital theme, they seek a new partner with whom they can build a new marriage around a new theme. It happens all the time. Surely you are familiar with couples who were divorced after meeting their goal of having children, building their dream home, finishing grad school, getting their careers off the ground, or a host of other time-limited goals, the fruits of which could easily be shared with a second husband or wife.

But a marital imperative is a marital theme, the ultimate goal of which takes a lifetime to achieve and which cannot be attained without the help of one, uniquely qualified partner. The specific goals related to a marital imperative, such as increasing personal competence, becoming more loving, being emotionally stronger, being more generous, take a lifetime to actualize. This leads to an incredible amount of fidelity and longevity in a marriage.

Designing Your Own Marital Imperative

Take a few moments to consider the type of person you want to be when you "grow up" and how your marriage can help you become that person. By the end of this exercise, you will have the beginnings of your own marital imperative.

Your Identity

Completing the entire exercise may take time. Don't try to rush through it, as you are going to be developing what amounts to the blueprint for the next fifty years of your life and marriage. Thoroughly meditate on all of the following questions. Do not share your answers with your mate at this time. This first part is about your identity, the identity which you would be responsible for living out whether or not you were ever married.

1. Of the values and ideals listed below, which are dearest to your heart? Identify a few virtues that are most important to you. Use the list below, or write your own ideas in the space provided. (If you have a hard time answering, try thinking of the qualities you wish to be most known for at the end of your life.)

__Love	__Faith	__Hope	__Personal Strength
__Understanding	__Wisdom	__Integrity	__Attentiveness
__Competence	__Moderation	__Charity	__Joy
__Peace	__Patience	__Kindness	__Goodness
__Generosity	__Gentleness	__Faithfulness	__Self-Control
__Service	__Hospitality	__Compassion	__Creativity
__Availability	__Good Humor	__Mercy	__Even-Temper

Others (list): _____

2. Write the virtues you indicated in the form of a personal motto. (For example: "I want to spend my life pursuing love, wisdom, and service.")

_____

_____

3a. Recall the things that irritate you most about your spouse: annoying habits, traits, infuriating opinions or behaviors. Write one or two of the most trying examples here.

_____

_____

3b. When your spouse does these annoying things, how, specifically, can you change your behavior to more adequately reflect your chosen motto. (For example: "How can I respond more lovingly when my spouse is late?")

_____

_____

4. We all hold back from our mates. What do you hold back? How will the qualities you identified help you overcome this selfishness? How will you motivate yourself to give more generously to your mate?

_____

_____

5a. What goals or accomplishments must you achieve if you are to become the person you wish to be by the end of your life? (Think of those most heartfelt desires that you have dismissed as silly but that somehow won't go away.)

_____

_____

5b. Do you have all the resources you need to accomplish these goals? If not, what do you need (more schooling, counseling, a different job, particular life experiences)?

_____

_____

6. What steps must you take so that your work, parenting, and personal life can more adequately reflect your personal motto (for example, take a parenting class, go on a couple's retreat, go to counseling, do more spiritual reading, get additional job training)?

_____

_____

Try the following to help you get a better idea what living out these particular qualities means in your unique set of circumstances. Imagine the "new improved you" (or an admired, imaginary big brother or sister). Pretend that this person exhibits all of the qualities you wish to develop in your life. In your mind's eye, see this person going through your day, handling all your problems and challenges in a manner that is consistent with the qualities and principles you have chosen. Then, step into this movie and allow yourself to feel what it is like to respond to your world in such a graceful manner. Watch this movie every day in the morning and once again at night to help you visualize the kind of person you are working toward becoming.

Your Partnership

You and you mate should now share and discuss your answers to the identity questions. You may want to do this in the setting of a "couple's retreat" (for example, at a weekend retreat or other quiet place). During this discussion keep in mind that your mate has arrived at his or her answers through careful reflection, and these answers reflect genuine beliefs about the identity he or she is responsible for fulfilling over a lifetime. This identity may involve things you don't appreciate, think are silly, or don't like, but this is irrelevant. To be faithful to your marriage vows is to be faithful to the purpose and function of marriage: helping each other become all that you were created to be. Discussing the following issues will help assure that you and your mate are a good influence on each other.

1. Develop your marital imperative. Review the personal mottos you and your mate developed in the identity part of this exercise. Now, combine those qualities into one statement that expresses the mission your marriage will seek to fulfill.

"As a couple, we will actively look for opportunities to increase our abilities to be…"

2. In order to be more faithful to your marital imperative, what changes do you need to make in the way you communicate and relate to each other? Do you have the emotional or relational skills to make these changes? If not to what resources (counseling, self-help reading, churches or other values groups) will you turn to acquire these skills?

3. How would your priorities as a couple need to shift in order to live up to your marital imperative? If there are serious changes to be made, sketch out a "five-year plan" of the steps you will take to make these changes.

Make a promise: You and your mate should now take turns extending the following promise to one another.

(Say your partner's name), I genuinely respect who you are as a person. I promise that I will work to see the good in the things that are important to you, especially when I don't understand. I will never belittle what is important to you. I will never say that your values, ideals, or goals are silly or unworthy of my time. I promise you that even as I am pursuing the goals that are most important to me—as I must—I will do all I can to help you become the person you wish to be at the end of your life.

I want to be the most important influence in your life. I promise to be the influence that helps you become the most complete, contented, and fulfilled person you can be, even when doing so challenges me or makes me uncomfortable. I promise you this because I love and honor who you are and what you are becoming. I will work for your good with all of my life, for all the days of my life.

A Marital Imperative: A Matter of Life and Death

In *The Good Marriage* (1995), Dr. Judith Wallerstein noted that one group of exceptional couples, those she calls Romantic marriages, were much more likely to have experienced the death of a parent than couples in her other categories. Considering that this was such a common experience for Romantic marriages, and since these couples were in many ways the most admirable relationships in her study, she theorized that the loss they suffered must have in some way contributed to the uncommon intimacy these husbands and wives shared. How can this be? While Dr. Wallerstein left this an open question, I believe the answer lies in the fact that these couples were forced to consider their own mortality and, like Shelby and Max, thought long and hard about the meaning they wanted to give to their own lives.

Most people spend a good deal of energy denying that one day they will die. The common perception is that time flows forward from birth and ends with a huge question mark at death—a view that makes life meaningless and absurd. But this is a mistake. I believe it was the philosopher Martin Heidegger who asserted that time flows backward from death giving life its meaning. Death clarifies. The person who is conscious of the reality of death is compelled to pursue meaning over entertainment, truth over trivialities, and actualization over mere activity. Faced with his or her own end, the only healthy response a person can make is, "I have important work to do and only a certain amount of time in which to do it. Let's not piddle around."

While many "naturally occurring" Exceptional couples may have had no choice but to confront both their mortality and the meaning of their lives, anyone who "begins with the end in mind"—as Stephen Covey puts it in *The Seven Habits of Highly Effective Families*—can benefit from the clarity of purpose and intimacy that results from asking the question, "What qualities do I wish to exhibit in my life and marriage and what would I need to do differently to be a better example of those ideals today?"

The work you did in the preceding exercise was intended to help you develop and clarify your marital imperative, but it was only a beginning. A true marital imperative is developed and expanded upon over the course of a lifetime. Review your plan every day as a way of checking your performance as a spouse against your perception of your performance as a spouse. And don't be afraid to regularly discuss your progress as a couple. Doing this will help you anticipate and resolve problems even before they are upon you.

Now that you have taken some time to clarify what you wish your life and marriage to be about, let's examine Exceptional Fidelity, the quality that will help you and your mate remain faithful to your marital imperative.

4

Exceptional Fidelity

It is better to be faithful than famous.
—THEODORE ROOSEVELT

IMAGINE THAT one day you come home and trip over a bump in your front yard. Irritated, you get a shovel and try to excise the offending lawn tumor. All at once, there is a thud as your shovel hits wood. "What the…?" you wonder as you continue to dig.

Suddenly, you realize that you have unearthed what appears to be a treasure chest. Returning hurriedly from the garage after getting a hammer and chisel, you break open the padlock, raise the lid, and discover an amazing cache of jewels and gold.

Do you simply leave the open treasure chest lying around in your yard for anyone to steal or do you bring it inside, guard it closely, and invest it wisely?

Marriage is the "yard bump" and many people spend their whole lives tripping over it. By developing your marital imperative, you discovered that "bump" is really a buried treasure. Now you have to make a choice. Do you shrug, say, "Hmm, treasure. Isn't that interesting…," pick up your newspaper off the stoop and close the door? Or, do you start planning all the wonderful ways your treasure is going to make your life richer and more fulfilling? Hopefully, you'll choose the latter, because this chapter is about investing your marital treasure wisely.

Most people think of fidelity in sexual terms as in, "I'm faithful to my spouse because I don't sleep around." But this is an incomplete definition at best. In his seminal book, *Childhood and Society* (1964), analyst Erik Erikson explained that fidelity was the virtue a person could claim after successfully resolving the struggle between "identity" and "role confusion." In other words, once a person has clarified the positive character traits he wishes to exemplify (that is, has an identity) that person is empowered to exhibit fidelity: to be faithful to those values, ideals, and goals in all aspects of his or her life. For Erikson, "fidelity" was another word for "identity strength."

Exceptional couples share this understanding of the word fidelity. To them, the promise to "forsake all others" includes all those entanglements, friendships, family-of-origin commitments, career opportunities, and community involvements that do not serve to increase either the physical and mental health of each spouse or the intimacy of the marriage. This kind of fidelity is absolutely essential if the marriage is to be a "partnership in destiny." I am not suggesting that to practice Exceptional Fidelity a husband and wife may never leave each other's side. Quite the contrary. What I am saying is that it raises the couple to a new level by empowering them to guard the intimate core of their marriage, encouraging them to prefer the meaningful companionship of a few close friends over a menagerie of casual acquaintances, and dispelling the illusion that social and occupational success must come at the price of marital poverty. Spouses in Exceptional marriages don't give up anything that is truly important. They just don't waste time pursuing anything that isn't.

Exceptional Fidelity is what gives a marital imperative its teeth. Without it, a marital imperative becomes a piece of paper you tape to your refrigerator door next to the calendar and underneath your grocery list. Once you and your mate have identified the values, ideals, and goals by which you wish to be defined, your own self-esteem requires you to go about the business of utilizing your marriage to faithfully live out those principles. Exceptional Fidelity facilitates this process in two ways. First, it helps you acknowledge your marriage as the most important work you do. Second, it puts you on the road to simplifying your life which, you will recall, is one of the hallmarks of Exceptional couplehood. Let's take a brief look at each.

Your Marriage: The Most Important Work

Life is filled with many interesting and important things to do, and pursuing Exceptional Fidelity in no way undermines the value of meaningful work, our need to give something back to our communities, or our responsibility to be generous and hospitable to our family and friends. What Exceptional Fidelity does is assert that there is no work more important than that of actualizing the values, ideals, and goals that are nearest and dearest to our hearts, and that there is no relationship more suited to this task than marriage. Exceptional Fidelity allows you to take advantage of the actualizing potential of even the simplest interactions between you and your mate. As a former client said after she and her husband began practicing their marital imperative, "I never appreciated how much I could grow by concentrating on the simple things. Giving meaningful kisses, really listening when Tom [her husband] talks, taking the time to ask questions rather than just report the events of my own day, are all such little things, but they really take effort when I'm tired, busy, or have a lot on my mind. If I wasn't being mindful of our marital imperative, I know I'd forget to do them at all. But when I make that effort, I come out of myself just a little bit. I feel closer to Tom, and then I see that in a small way, I really am becoming more of that peaceful, thoughtful person I want to be."

A marital imperative raises your marriage from an institution of convenience and companionship and enables it to become an instrument for actualization. Of course you can be loving, generous, wise, strong, and creative outside of your marriage. By all means you must. But marriage offers you many more opportunities to fulfill those qualities than any other outlet. No one else knows you as well as your mate; no one else sees you in as many contexts as your mate. Therefore, no one else is as qualified as your mate to help you achieve the congruence between your life and values that is necessary for true identity strength, and ultimately, true joy.

Exceptional Fidelity: The Road to Simplification

Once you have designed your marital imperative, Exceptional Fidelity compels you to examine your life with one question in mind, "Are the roles I play and the people with whom I associate helping or hindering my desire to fulfill the values, ideals, and goals that are central to my ultimate happiness?"

Carl, a former sales representative for a major manufacturing company, found that asking this question helped him reclaim his life and marriage. As he says, "My marital imperative [developed with his wife, Erica] helped me see that relationships had a purpose beyond how they were making me feel in that moment. I started noticing that some of my friends weren't as supportive of my values as others, and I realized that if I was ever going to come close to living out the principles Erica and I established for our marriage, I needed to find a different place to work." Carl started by sitting down with Erica at breakfast and scheduling some time together every day. Whatever time was left he divided between his hobbies and his closest friends, significantly decreasing the time he spent with simple acquaintances. Finally, through persistent effort, Carl was able to find a position in a smaller company. It required him to take a small pay cut, but as he said, "The time with Erica and the kids combined with the less stressful environment more than makes up for the money."

Sherry is another example of how Exceptional Fidelity allows you to simplify your life, giving you more energy to pursue your own growth and marital bliss. Married to Todd for five years, Sherry is a real estate broker who gets a great deal of pleasure from both her work and her relationship with her coworkers. She felt close to one woman in particular, Angela, who was very needy, and who managed to entangle herself in a series of destructive relationships. Angela would frequently call Sherry late in the evening, begging Sherry to meet her and talk her through her latest crisis. When Todd finally complained about the increasingly frequent intrusions into their life, Sherry accused him of trying to monopolize her time and rushed to Angela's side despite Todd's irritation. As Sherry put it, "I thought I was doing the right thing by trying to be there for my friend." But after the couple clarified their marital imperative in session with me, Sherry had an interesting insight. "Intimacy doesn't come easily to me," she said, "and I'm starting to see how I've been using Angela's crises as a way to keep Todd at a distance." As the counseling progressed, Sherry began to understand how she and Todd needed each other on a deeper level and that their relationship would only become what it could be if she asserted its priority to Angela. While this deeper intimacy frightened her—due to some events in her past—she also understood what she was missing and was eager to do the work necessary to overcome her limitations. Practicing Exceptional Fidelity in Sherry's case meant both pushing through her fear of intimacy and, while not cutting off Angela entirely, setting restrictions on the frequency of Angela's calls, who, after some initial protests, found another woman to latch on to.

Exceptional Fidelity can be very difficult for Conventional couples, who tend to confuse who they are with the work they do and the roles they play. Often, they take offense when I suggest they cut back on their work schedules and community involvements for the sake of themselves and their marriage. They say, "But you said I should be true to myself. I really love my work." Recently, I had a very telling conversation with an account manager for an advertising agency. When she learned what I did for a living she told me that, due to her long hours and frequent travel, she was having problems with her children, with whom she felt out of touch. Also, she had frequent migraine headaches, due to stress, according to her doctor, and she suffered from mild panic attacks and insomnia because she couldn't get work off her mind. When I suggested that her work, or at least her schedule, didn't agree with her, she looked at me in shocked surprised, "But I love what I do!"

It is easy to become addicted to the adrenaline rush that accompanies a harried life. For many people, "harried" is synonymous with "needed." And the more crazed you feel, the more special you are. Of course, the more a person follows this recipe for "self-esteem" the more he or she begins to fall apart—the logical consequence of pursuing mere activity over actualization.

But what about people who really believe that the work they do affords more opportunities for actualizing their value systems? What about people who believe, perhaps with good reason, that their careers or causes prevent them from being more active participants in married life? Raymond is a physician who works over seventy hours per week. He is married to Amanda, a radiological technician, and I was seeing both of them for marriage counseling—as schedules permitted. In response to Amanda's complaints in session about his work hours, Raymond exclaimed, "I need to be available to my patients. I love you, but my work is really life and death. What am I supposed to do, say, 'I'm sorry your husband died, Mrs. Smith, but I needed to take my wife to the movies.'"

Likewise, several years ago, I did some phone consultations with a woman from Oregon whose husband, in addition to his work, was very active in the environmental movement. So active, in fact, that he was away from home most weekends and several nights per week. She didn't begrudge him his passion, and she had her own interests in addition to their three children. She simply never saw her husband. When she would try to talk to him about his absences, he would nod sympathetically and say, "I know, Hon. I wish I could be home more, but you know how important this is."

Both Dr. Raymond and our environmentalist friend have a point, at least superficially. Saving lives and saving the environment are important. Very important. But if being true to yourself means giving yourself entirely to a cause or a career, then what are you doing being married? Let me put it this way. Imagine going to the pet store and buying a dog. Would you then take it home, lock it in the basement and starve it to death? What kind of a person would that make you? Would you be justified in saying, "I didn't know I had to feed and water it?" Would saying, "But I had to be out saving the world" let you off the hook? Of course not. If it is shocking to do this to an animal, how much more shocking is it to promise to care for your mate's soul and then starve it to death through inattention? What kind of a person does that make you—worthwhile though your career and causes may be?

If a person has a calling to give his life totally to a cause, career, or ministry, then I sincerely congratulate him on his noble, selfless vocation—and wish him well in his life of celibacy. But when you marry, you accept certain responsibilities, the first of which is to care for the soul of your mate—and vice versa. Being true to yourself does not mean running yourself into an early grave, like our advertising executive, or running around saving the world, like our doctor and our activist. It means finding a way to balance all the promises and commitments you have made, whether they be to a spouse, children, employers, family, community, or friends. And, when your plate is too full, if it is not possible to balance all those commitments, Exceptional Fidelity gives you permission to scale back or even eliminate those nonmarital commitments which are least helpful to fulfilling the values, ideals, and goals upon which your life and marriage are based.

Good Fences Make Good Marriages

It is the job of every couple to determine for themselves how much time and energy they can give to important others without violating the primacy of their marriage. In this sense, Exceptional Fidelity is the art of setting respectful boundaries (that is, being able to respectfully determine where your responsibilities end and another person's begin). A person is said to have "good boundaries" if she is able to be generous to others without being a doormat. Boundaries protect the dignity of the person, the importance of the marital imperative, and the primacy of the marriage over all other relationships. When a person is unable to set appropriate boundaries, she experiences a great deal of confusion and stress as all the people she knows and roles she occupies compete to receive the lion's share of her time and energy. The individual's mental health and intimate relationship suffer while she runs around pell-mell trying to please everyone and failing miserably. The following pages will give you a starting point for maintaining healthy, respectful boundaries in your life and marriage.

Step 1: Practice "Marriage First"

Every day is a new opportunity to renew your wedding vows. When you give your mate his or her good morning kiss, I would encourage you to tell your mate (or at least think to yourself), "Today, I'm going to say, 'I do' all over again, by considering our marriage in every choice I make."

Beyond this, each morning, remind yourself of your marital imperative. Remember that it is based upon the values that support your identity. Because of this, your ultimate success as a person is dependent upon your ability to work toward your marital impera- tive—and protect the primacy of your marriage—today. When your marriage is founded on a marital imperative, you cannot be replaced. Nor can your spouse be replaced with anyone else because each of you plays a unique role in fulfilling each other's identities. No request or demand another person can make of you is worth betraying your pursuit of actualization—becoming the person you want to be between now and the day you die. As you go through your day, keep your marriage in the forefront of your mind and look for ways to let your mate know how important his or her presence is to your life.

Step 2: Make Your Marital Imperative the Standard for Weighing Requests

Sometimes parents, employers, or friends make requests of us that may seem perfectly reasonable to them but are completely inappropriate as far as our own lives are concerned. Setting respectful boundaries (that is, practicing Exceptional Fidelity) requires you to be able to give when it is appropriate to give and say "no" when it is appropriate. This is difficult for many people because they have no objective standard against which to weigh requests from others. Lacking this standard, they tend to rely on their feelings to tell them what to do. This leads to all sorts of problems.

For example, some people feel like they can never refuse others. Saying "no" to even an inappropriate request raises feelings of almost unbearable guilt.

Deanne, a mother of two, felt a compelling need to spend several hours a day visiting with her mother. She also frequently ran errands for her mother, who was in no way infirm but simply preferred to not go out of the house if she could help it. The problem was that Deanne, a freelance writer, didn't have enough time to get her own work done, much less make time for her husband and children, all of whom were suffering from her absence. Even though she admitted this, she felt horribly guilty when she even thought about refusing her mother. Actually, this guilt extended to other circumstances as well. She frequently volunteered to baby-sit for her sister and made herself the arbiter of squabbles between her siblings and her parents, even though she had time for none of this. Her motto was, "I have to do it, because nobody else will."

Deanne was eventually forced to seek treatment for the panic attacks that resulted from her inability to stand up to her guilt feelings. Only after she clarified her own mission statement and began living it out was she able to set limits on her generosity in order to reclaim both her sanity and her marriage. The same was true for Miki, a woman whose life defined the phrase "work ethic." Her desire to do the best job possible for her employer included regularly staying at the office until ten or eleven o'clock at night to complete the work her boss would hand her when he left for home at three in the afternoon. Needless to say, this exacted a heavy toll on her marriage. She came to me feeling torn between her important work and her relationship, which was deteriorating rapidly.

And then there are other people who feel as though they have to constantly guard themselves against being taken advantage of. They have absolutely no problem saying "no." In fact, their problem is that they never say "yes."

Frank grew up in a home where his needs were rarely, if ever, respected. Because of this, he developed a very "in your face" arguing style, especially with his wife. When she asked for more time or attention from him, his refusals were immediate, especially when there was something he wanted to do. As he put it, "I've lived my whole life doing what other people told me to do. I'll be damned if I'm going to let my wife control me."

It should be obvious that neither position is healthy. You cannot base decisions to give or withhold service based solely on how you feel about it. But you can respond to requests from people rationally and respectfully, asking yourself one question, "Would responding positively to this request cause me to be more, or less, faithful to my marital imperative?"

Basing your responses on your marital imperative helps you achieve an objective, respectful balance. It helps you rationally say "yes" when you ought to say "yes," and "no" when you ought to say "no." And because these decisions are rational and healthy, it is more difficult—in fact, almost impossible—to be guilted out of them.

Setting Boundaries

The following pages will help you examine how well you use boundaries to practice Exceptional Fidelity in several specific areas of your life.

At Work

Of all the areas where boundaries are needed, for most people, this is the most difficult place to set them. The rewards for not setting boundaries (for example, money, the approval of employers and coworkers for being ambitious, promotions, titles) are often too appealing to resist. In order to help you see if you are making an appropriate use of boundaries in your work life, take the following true-false quiz.

<u>WORK BOUNDARIES QUIZ</u>

T   F   I feel more rewarded by my work than I do my marriage and family life.

T   F   I am often thinking about work when I'm home.

T   F   My spouse and I regularly argue about our work schedules.

T   F   I use my job as a way of escaping the craziness of my home life.

T   F   I regularly have to break dates with my spouse or miss family events due to my work.

Answering "true" to any one of these may warrant your thinking about ways to improve your use of boundaries in your work life.

Answering "true" to three or more items may indicate the need for more serious attention: A job change, counseling, or other interventions may be appropriate. Discuss this with your mate.

With Friends

We all need friends. But sometimes, our friends need us too much. A true friend must be supportive and respectful of your marriage. He or she must not attempt to compete with it—intentionally or unintentionally—nor should he or she be privy to information you do not tell your mate. Take the following true-or-false quiz to see if you are making an appropriate use of boundaries with your friends.

<u>FRIENDSHIP BOUNDARY QUIZ</u>

T   F   I have one or more friends who are constantly in crisis and I always feel obliged to run to their aid.

T   F   My spouse complains about the amount of time I spend with my friends.

T   F   I think of my friends as the people I go out with to escape the craziness of my marriage or family life.

T   F   I tell my friends things I would never tell my mate.

T   F   I feel closer to some of my friends than I do my spouse.

Answering "true" to any one of these may warrant your thinking about ways to improve your use of boundaries in your social life.

Answering "true" to three or more items may indicate the need for more serious attention: Rethinking certain relationships, counseling (for your marriage or yourself), or other interventions may be appropriate. Discuss this with your mate.

With Family of Origin

Our parents will always be important to us, but when they compete for first place with your own marriage, they have become too important. Take the following true-or-false quiz to see if you are making appropriate use of boundaries with your family of origin.

FAMILY-OF-ORIGIN BOUNDARY QUIZ

T   F   I often feel torn between my mate and my parents.

T   F   There are no secrets between my parents and me. I tell them everything that goes on between my spouse and me.

T   F   I probably spend more time with my parents than with my mate.

T   F   My mate complains about the amount of involvement my parents have in our lives.

T   F   I feel too guilty to ever say "no" to my parents.

Answering "true" to any one of these may warrant your thinking about ways to improve your use of boundaries with your family of origin.

Answering "true" to three or more items may indicate the need for more serious attention: Rethinking your relationship with your parents, counseling (for your marriage or yourself), or other interventions may be appropriate. Discuss this with your mate.

In Other Social Areas

Giving back to our community, supporting causes, and generally "being involved" are very important for our mental health. However, if these things compete with our marriages, they can just as easily be a source of grief. Take the following true-or-false quiz to see if you are making an appropriate use of boundaries in the other social aspects of your life.

SOCIAL BOUNDARIES QUIZ

T F My social commitments regularly cut into time with my spouse and children.

T F I use my social involvements as a way to escape the craziness of my marriage and family life.

T F My mate complains about the amount of time my social commitments are taking from our marriage.

T F I feel too guilty to say "no" when people ask me to volunteer for committees or various projects.

T F I feel more rewarded by my social and community involvements than I do my marriage and family life.

Answering "true" to any one of these may warrant your thinking about ways to improve your use of boundaries in your social engagements.

Answering "true" to three or more items may indicate the need for more serious attention: Rethinking your community involvements, counseling (for your marriage or yourself), or other interventions may be appropriate. Discuss this with your mate.

What About Setting Boundaries With My Mate?

Exceptional Fidelity does not only refer to your ability to protect the integrity of your marriage. It also refers to your ability to protect your own integrity *within* your marriage. Because of this, it will sometimes be necessary to set boundaries with your mate, especially when you are not sure how a particular request he or she has made is consistent with your principles. Since this issue touches on several facets of married life, I will address boundary setting within the marriage in several different chapters. Chapters 5 and 6 cover boundaries and their relationship to love and marital service, chapter 8 discusses setting healthy boundaries in arguments, and chapter 11 addresses sexual boundaries.

The next exercise will enable you and your mate to have a clear and mutual sense of your priorities. This way, when conflicts arise between two areas of your life, you can make efficient choices about what to attend to first. To help clarify the importance of the various people, organizations, institutions, and activities with which you are involved, take a moment, grab a pen and paper, and complete the following.

ESTABLISHING YOUR PRIORITIES

1. Including your spouse and children, list the most important people in your life with whom you and your mate have regular dealings.
2. List the activities with which you are involved (include work).
3. List all the activities you are not currently involved in, but hope to become active in soon (for example, school, a church group, political organization).
4. Now, rank all the people and activities you listed above in the order of importance they play in your pursuit of your marital imperative. Force yourself to write only one item on each space (although you may combine certain items into general categories like "family" or "coworkers").

Discuss the following with your mate.

1. If you and your mate were to actually live by the order of priorities you listed, what changes would you have to make in your life?
2. How might these changes benefit your marriage?
3. What could you do to begin making these changes possible?

Post your list where you and your mate will see it. When conflicts between two items on your priority list arise, try your best to give more weight to the higher-ranked item.

Overdraft Protection

By helping us define and protect our priorities, Exceptional Fidelity prevents our emotional bank accounts from becoming overdrawn. When I was a young child, I used to think that checks were magical things. If my parents said they didn't have enough money to buy me a toy, I would say, "Can't you write a check?" I had no idea that my parents' bank account was, indeed, a very finite resource.

In the same way, we humans are finite creatures with access to finite social, psychological, and emotional resources. Every role we play, every relationship we enter into "costs" a certain amount of those resources, leaving us with less to "spend" on other roles and relationships. Just like buying too many items on credit is poor financial management, entering into too many relationships and roles without the emotional resources to pay for them is poor self-management. We must spend wisely, concentrating primarily on our needs and most important wants first. Everything else is gravy.

Some expenditures are just that. We spend ourselves and feel drained for the effort. Other expenditures, like having a rewarding marriage and family life, are really investments that pay dividends for a lifetime. In the treasure chest metaphor that began the chapter, you had to expend some effort to dig up the "married treasure," but weren't you glad you did?

In a world filled with truly wonderful opportunities around every corner, there are those who question the wisdom of asserting the priority of one's marriage over everything else. Of course, if marriage is just another source of companionship, then asserting its priority makes absolutely no sense at all. But if your marriage is built around a marital imperative, then it is your best hope for actualizing all the values, ideals, and goals which are important to you. Nothing could be more important than that.

Besides being the source of your identity strength, Exceptional Fidelity empowers you to assert the beauty and importance of your marriage to the world at large and reminds you and your mate to constantly reassure each other's value, specialness, and dignity. Exceptional Fidelity provides the safety and marital integrity necessary for the next quality we are going to examine: Exceptional Loving.

5

Exceptional Loving

All those who have good... wives [and] husbands...,
may be sure that at some times... they are loved not
because they are lovable but because Love himself is in
those who love them.

—C. S. LEWIS

You can be certain you truly love someone if (choose one):

A. You feel warmly toward him/her.
B. You wouldn't be able to survive without him/her.
C. You really enjoy his/her company.
D. You can just be together without having to say a word.
E. You have a great sex life.
F. All of the above.
G. None of the above.

The correct answer is G, none of the above. A, C, and D are all various types of affection, and while affection is one way love manifests itself, it is much too passive to represent the fullness of real love. On the other hand, E implies passion, which is also an important part of marital love, but most of us are very familiar with examples of romance without substance and chemistry without commitment to confuse mere passion with "the real thing." Finally, B is a fairly good definition of simple dependency, a quality which is the antithesis of love. Dependency quickly poisons relationships. In fact, the more dependency there is in a relationship the more likely that relationship will be unsatisfactory or short-lived.

So what is love anyway? And how do you know if you are in it?

Each couple along the Relationship Pathway has their own definition of love. For example, couples in Deadly marriages tend not to think too much about love. They are looking for a good time, a distraction, and the relationship will last as long as the couple can provide this escape for each other.

Shipwrecked couples tend to think of love as a feeling that happens to them, a mystery with a life of its own. These couples often balk at suggestions that a good relationship takes work ("A good relationship should just happen, you shouldn't have to work so hard"), or that lost feelings of love can be regained ("I just don't *feel* it, I don't know if it will ever come back"). To them, you're either in love or you aren't, and "working" on getting love back just feels dishonest ("I can't be loving to him if I don't *feel* it. That would just be leading him on").

Conventional couples do a pretty good job of defining love. They have at least a fair understanding that love is really a kind of work. They tend to think of love not only in terms of good feelings, but also in terms of respect and mutual "taking care of." The only difficulty is that in a Conventional marriage, love tends to be limited by the greater value the couple places on "fairness" or "equity" (see chapter 2). As long as the balance of domestic labor and the balance of power remain about equal, as long as both husband and wife feel as though each is making a more or less equal emotional and psychological contribution to the marriage, all is well. But if for any reason this equity is threatened by one spouse, the other spouse's defenses go up ("I'll be loving as long as it's safe, but I'm not going to be taken advantage of either").

And then there are the couples who fall into the Exceptional marriage category, for whom true love is nothing less than desiring and working toward the good of another—every single moment of every single day, whether they feel like doing the work or not. Exceptional couples enjoy the pleasant emotions that accompany the work of love, and they certainly enjoy being taken care of, but, more than anything, Exceptional couples know that love is not a feeling. It is a choice. It is work. It is an exercise of the will by which they are perfected. Exceptional couples do not think of their marriage as a labor of love. They think of love as the labor required of marriage. They know that being a loving person means more than thinking fondly of your mate, having warmness in your heart for him, being good at saying "the love words," or even doing loving things when the power-dynamic is equal and one feels like doing them. For the Exceptional spouse, love is *choice* and *action*. It is getting up in the morning and asking, "What can I do to make my mate's life easier, more pleasant, or more fulfilling today?" For the partners in an Exceptional couple, love is daily making choices with one's mate in mind, setting a schedule with one's marriage in mind, and planning a future with the marital imperative in mind—not because they necessarily feel like it, but because to do less is offensive to their personal dignity. Furthermore, in Exceptional marriages, love is not affected by scorekeeping because being loving is not something to be done for the sake of one's spouse. It is done for the sake of one's self. The Exceptional spouse holds himself or herself responsible for being loving, whether his or her mate deserves such generosity or not, because that is the kind of person he or she wants to be when he or she grows up. To be less than loving is to do violence to one's self-concept. This is the essence of what I refer to as Exceptional Loving.

The Four Mysteries of Exceptional Loving Revealed

Exceptional couples understand the four mysteries of Exceptional Loving. They are as follows:

1. Exceptional Love is an "individual act of the will."
2. Exceptional Love is an action that drives emotion.
3. Exceptional Love mixes 75 percent companionate love with 25 percent romantic love.
4. Exceptional Love is the means to actualization.

Like Exceptional Fidelity (see chapter 4), Exceptional Love is not so much a quality as it is a skill that must be practiced and perfected. The following pages will illuminate the four mysteries of exceptional loving and give you a chance find those opportunities for love which you may currently be missing out on.

1. Exceptional Love Is an Individual Act of the Will

If thou must love me, let it be for naught
Except for love's sake only.

—ELIZABETH BARRETT BROWNING

Many good things in relationships involve feelings. Passion is a feeling. Affection is a feeling, as are fondness and attraction. But love "for love's sake" is not a feeling. It is an individual act of the will. To love "for love's sake only" is to love someone for the express purpose of practicing your skills as a lover and being perfected by that love as you work for the good of your partner.

Exceptional Loving is the fuel that propels the Exceptional couple to their ultimate destination—actualization. Now, this statement makes absolutely no sense if love is simply a feeling. How could something as transient as an emotion, a mere chemical by-product of the limbic system, spur a person—much less a couple—on to actualization? The fact is, it can't. Love can only be an actualizing event if it is Exceptional Love, that is, if it is a love which is not merely a feeling, but rather a commitment to desire and work toward the good of another—whether or not one *feels* like doing so.

Regardless of whether one feels wonderfully about the other on any given day, the Exceptional spouse will seek out opportunities to work for his or her mate's good and search for ways to demonstrate the other's specialness, not necessarily because the mate deserves such generosity but because to act in any other way is beneath the spouse's own dignity. This deeply personal commitment to loving action exemplifies true love as an individual act of the will.

No doubt there are those of you who are thinking, "That sounds kind of codependent to me." You are expressing a legitimate concern. Acting lovingly toward someone who does not necessarily deserve such generosity (that is, practicing "sacrificial love") could be the act of a codependent person, or it could be the act of a very mature person. It all depends on one thing: a balance between both sensitivity and personal strength in the character of the lover. A codependent person uses sacrificial love in an indiscriminate and manipulative way. She attaches herself to someone who cannot love her back and then "loves" him with all her might in a fruitless attempt to save him, so that he, someday, will save her. She expects nothing from her beloved and gets even less. In the course of this melodrama, she may subject herself to all sorts of abuse, neglect, and humiliation all in the name of something she will call "love" but which is completely undeserving of the name. By contrast, the mature lover using sacrificial love expects—in fact, requires—the person receiving the love to respond. She is simply willing to extend a bit of emotional credit and take the first step when necessary. For example, she might be willing to be the first to say "I'm sorry" in an argument even if both were wrong, or she might be willing to make some very difficult sacrifices for the sake of her mate. But if this imbalance were to persist for a period of several weeks, or if her sacrifices were to go unnoticed or unappreciated, she would be just as comfortable addressing his neglect, and he would most likely be grateful being told about it and make the appropriate corrections—because he also desires to be an exceptional lover. If codependency is sensitivity in the absence of personal strength, then healthy sacrificial love demonstrates the balance between sensitivity and personal strength.

The following quiz can help you see if you have what it takes to use sacrificial love in a healthy way.

Choose "T" for true or "F" for false according to how each statement applies to the way you act in your marriage.

TEST FOR PERSONAL STRENGTH

T   F   My life reflects a clear set of values (that is, "I don't have to say, 'I believe such and such.' You can tell by looking at my life.")

T   F   I am capable of providing for my own needs (emotional/financial).

T   F   I enjoy being by myself.

T   F   I have strong opinions.

T   F   I am comfortable in conflict (though I don't look for fights).

T   F   I am not easily intimidated.

T   F   I am not slighted or offended easily.

T   F   My own satisfaction/fulfillment is important to me.

T   F   Certain things are worth fighting for.

T   F   I speak my mind.

TEST FOR SENSITIVITY

T   F   I am careful not to offend others with my speech or actions.

T   F   I am quick to notice another person's pain.

T   F   I go out of my way to help others in need.

T   F   I am a good listener.

T   F   People tell me I'm easy to talk to (or everybody seems to talk to me).

T   F   Being considerate is very important to me.

T   F   I am concerned about the happiness of others.

T   F   I believe that the people I know are basically good-hearted.

T   F   It would be very painful for me to lose a friend.

T   F   I am comfortable talking about my feelings.

Compare your scores for both parts of the quiz.

• If you answered "true" to six or more statements in both Personal Strength and Sensitivity it suggests that you probably have the skills to use sacrificial love in the healthiest possible way.

• Answering "true" to fewer than six statements in both Personal Strength and Sensitivity suggests that you aren't remarkably sensitive nor do you have much strength of character. You may run the risk of not caring enough about anything—including your own personal growth—to make sacrificial love seem worthwhile to you. You need to develop some passions and a greater concern for others if you want more than a perpetually stagnant life and marriage.

• A high score (6+) in Personal Strength combined with a low score (5−) in Sensitivity suggests that sacrificial love does not come easy to you. Depending upon the disparity between the two scores, you may tend to come across as either selfish or a bully. Work on your awareness of other's feelings and perceptions of you. Being right all of the time is no fun if it eventually causes you to be alone all of the time.

• A low score (5−) in Personal Strength combined with a high score (6+) in Sensitivity suggests that you may have a tendency toward being a doormat instead of using sacrificial love in a healthy way. Depending on the disparity between these two scores, you may also have some codependent tendencies. Find something to believe in—starting with yourself—and stand up for it.

By learning how to use sacrificial love in a healthy manner, the Exceptional lover is able to choose his battles wisely and sacrifice when necessary for the common good. In this way, love as an individual act of the will is never codependent. It is a means of actualization.

2. Exceptional Loving Is an Action That Drives Emotion

Married eleven years, Valerie and Thomas weren't sure whether they wanted to stay married. It seemed that the good feelings had gone out of their marriage. After I explained to them how love is an act of the will, Valerie challenged me with the question, "Aren't you asking us to lie? I mean, if I don't feel loving, how can I be loving? That's just being dishonest with my feelings."

It is not dishonest to *be* loving when you don't *feel* loving. In fact, for love to be true love, you must be able to be loving especially when you don't feel like it, otherwise what you are calling "love" is simply emotional masturbation. In other words, if you only love when you feel like it, then love is not something done for the good of another, but for your own pleasure. Ultimately, such "love" produces nothing except a shallow sense of self-satisfaction.

In chapter 3, I sang the praises of congruence. Many readers may be wondering why I might now seem to be contradicting myself. After all, isn't acting in a manner that is inconsistent with one's emotions incongruent? This is an excellent question. Let me try to answer it this way. Congruence with one's value system—that is, making choices and plans according to one's values, ideals, and goals—is absolutely essential for mental health. On the other hand, congruence with one's emotions—that is, making choices and plans according to one's present emotional state—is a decidedly mixed bag.

For example, if you are angry at your mate, you should most likely tell him about it and work it out. This is an example of healthy emotional congruence. But let's say that for some reason your anger remains stuck in the "on" position even after you've worked it all out. Do you really think the healthy response to this is sitting around pouting, moping, and making your mate's life a living hell simply because you *feel* like it? Of course not. Likewise, if the clinically depressed person feels like killing himself, must he be "emotionally congruent" and do it? Of course not.

The truth is, a person must be faithful to, and congruent with, all of his or her rationally based emotions. So how do you tell if an emotion is rationally based? There are several ways, but the easiest is asking yourself the following question: "Will acting on this emotion make me more or less of the person I want to be when I grow up?" For example, let's say that one of the qualities you identified with in chapter 3 was "being a loving person." Let's further say that, for whatever reason, you woke up in a remarkably unloving mood (an almost daily occurrence for non–morning people like myself). On the one hand, your feelings are telling you to take a break from being loving, on the other hand, your value system says there is no such thing as "taking a break" from being loving. What to do? The healthy person will choose to follow his value system and be loving. Emotional congruence does not mean acting in a manner that is congruent with your emotions; it means being so congruent that even your emotions support your values, ideals, and goals. But getting to this point takes work. Specifically, it takes the work known as "fake it 'till you make it."

Despite how it sounds, faking it 'till you make it is not the same as lying. It is simply a kind of discipline. Once you have decided that your value system dictates a particular choice even though your emotions do not support that choice, faking it 'till you make it is the discipline that allows you to move past the point you are at today and become the person you want to be tomorrow.

Imagine that you are starting a new job. It's your first day and you are fairly nervous. Worse, you will be required to attend an important meeting with several top executives of the firm. Taking into account that you are so nervous that you feel like you are going to throw up any minute, how do you act? Do you go into the meeting stumbling over yourself, apologizing at every turn, and constantly looking at the small air-sickness bag you placed on the table in front of you "just in case"? Or do you take a breath, give yourself a pep talk and fake it 'till you make it? Of course, you'll choose the latter. But why would you choose to "mislead" your employers in such a way? Aren't you being dishonest? Of course not. You know the qualities you want to exhibit, so you project the desired image in the hopes that you will grow into it. You are practicing emotional congruence by training your emotions to be congruent with the image you have of your "true self," the self you want to be.

The same is true in relationships. Because Exceptional spouses want to be loving people, they project a loving image of themselves so that one day they can grow into that image. And a funny thing happens. When a couple makes a commitment to acting in loving ways whether they feel like it or not, paradoxically they end up feeling more and more in love: Loving feelings feed off of loving actions. The more loving things a person does for another, the more loving that person will feel toward the other. Let's use your relationship as an example.

Imagine that things are going well for you and your mate. You are focusing a great deal of energy on the relationship, you are spending time together, and you feel great about each other. But there is a problem: While you are focusing on your relationship, you have been spending less time focusing on the other responsibilities in your life, and they are beginning to suffer. Feeling secure about your relationship, you begin to attend to those other responsibilities, putting more energy into your work, social commitments, etc. Almost imperceptibly, you become less attuned to your relationship as you focus more energy on the other important areas of your life. Pretty soon, you find yourself at a low ebb in your marriage. You feel somewhat estranged from your mate. You begin sniping at each other over silly things and having meaningless arguments. Now you have a choice to make. You can either sit there in your bad feelings and let your relationship fall down around your ears because you don't feel like doing anything loving right now ("Why should I always have to be the one to blink first when we play marital chicken?") or you can realize that the reason you feel so unloving toward your mate is because you haven't been doing loving things for your mate. You've been too distracted. Let's say you choose the latter, the healthier, option. You decide to stop at the grocery store on your way home and pick up your spouse's favorite ice cream—one that you happen not to like—just to do something nice. You make an effort to let some of your mate's grumpy comments go by that evening, and instead work hard to be pleasant. Then you take out your calendar, look your mate in the eye and say, "I love being with you and we haven't had much time for each other lately. I really miss my best friend. Let's make a plan." Then you and your mate find a way to squeeze each other into your busy lives. Already the tension is melting. Suddenly, you are a team again. You are asserting the priority of your marriage to each other, the positive feelings are coming back, and you are beginning to look forward to that date, or whatever, that you planned together.

All of the things I cited in the above example are very simple and none too profound. But they have an enormous impact on the loving dynamic of a relationship. True love does not have to be dramatic to count, it just has to show effort and thought. Exceptional couples know that the secret to lasting love is making a daily effort to be aware of the simple details of caring for one another—whether they feel like it today or not. The paradox is, the more a couple does for each other, whether they feel like it or not, the more they feel like doing it. People don't ever "just fall out of love." They usually starve it to death by withholding loving actions while waiting around for their loving feelings to magically return. Unfortunately, "they" (loving feelings) never do because "they" have no life of their own, only the life you give them through your loving efforts to work for the good of your mate. When *you* stop, "they" stop. How can you avoid accidentally starving your love to death? Take a minute to complete the following exercise.

Twenty-five Ways to Make Love—Every Day

Successful marriages are nurtured every day in the little exchanges between two people. Major efforts (weekends away, extra-special surprises, etc.) are important, but tend to become less frequent as time goes by. Real love is played out in the simple consideration, playfulness, and attentiveness that a couple exhibits toward each other every day. Examples could include things as simple as making a point of sitting on the same piece of furniture together, kissing when you leave and enter a room, making eye contact when you talk to each other.

Make a list of twenty-five simple, daily things that your mate does—or that you would like him or her to do more of—that demonstrate regard for you. If you get stuck, try recalling the things other people do that help you feel listened to, cared for, or appreciated. In short, what simple things make you feel special when someone does them?

Ask your mate to put together a similar list. Then trade lists. Make yourself responsible for doing as many things on your mate's list as often as possible. See how many you can do every week.

I recommend making multiple copies of both of your lists and pasting them in all the obvious places: your bathroom mirror, the refrigerator, the dashboard of your car. This way, you can't forget, because you can't escape. Every day, be conscious of your behavior as a spouse. Loving your mate means working for his or her good specifically in the ways identified on the list. Everyone wants to be considered an exceptional lover by their spouse. How good a lover you are is directly dependent upon the number of the things you regularly do for your mate which can be found on your mate's list. For some of you, this will be a real reality check, for others, it will be a validation of all your hard work. Regardless, every single one of us can do better. What more can *you* do? What obstacles will you need to overcome in order to become a better lover to your mate? Will you need to learn some new skills? Will you need to learn to appreciate some activities you've been reluctant to try? Or to be more attentive? Granted, all this learning can make a person uncomfortable, but ultimately, these are the lessons you must practice on your road to actualizing yourself and fulfilling your marital imperative. I never said Exceptional Loving would be easy. I just promised that it would be worth it.

Doing something on your mate's "love list" every day is good practice in maintaining your marriage and fulfilling your own identity. Doing these things every day—whether you feel like it or not—will help you experience more highs in your relationship and fewer, and less threatening, lows. Finally, they will help you on your way to becoming the loving, generous person you want to be when you grow up.

3. Exceptional Love Is 75 Percent Friendship and 25 Percent Romance

The work of love manifests itself on two fronts: Companionate love (friendship) and romantic love (sexuality and sentiment). Of the two, companionate love should be the greater portion of the recipe for true love, making up about 70-80 percent of the total mixture. Romantic love should make up the remaining 20-30 percent. Let's look at each.

Companionate love is the work a couple does to maintain their basic friendship. It is the daily effort they put into sharing each other's worlds, learning about each other's interests, and sharing competencies. Companionate love must make up the center of a healthy relationship. It is companionate love that prevents a couple from growing apart; that pushes one to try new things because of their mate which they might have never tried on their own; that makes each spouse prefer doing *anything* as a couple over something he or she truly enjoys doing—with anyone else. The only problem with companionate love is that there isn't a great deal of feeling involved with it. The best label for the emotion that accompanies companionate love is "caring." While caring is extremely important to an Exceptional marriage, it lacks a certain passion, and without passion, a marriage can feel downright empty. And that's where romantic love comes in.

Romantic love is the work a couple does to assert their mutual attraction, specialness, and desirability to one another. It is knowing how to make one's mate feel like the uniquely fascinating person he or she is to you. Romantic love puts the "*Woo!*" into relationships. This having been said, you might wonder why it should make up only about 25 percent of the marital love mix. Simply for this reason: romantic love is too unstable to stand on its own. To be considered healthy, romantic love must flow from companionate love, not stand in place of it. In her book, *The Good Marriage,* Dr. Judith Wallerstein observes that as wonderful as romantic love can be, it "has the tragic potential for freezing the husband and wife into a self-absorbed, childlike preoccupation with each other, turning its back on the rest of the world, including the children."

Shipwrecked couples have a hard time with the balance between companionate and romantic loves. They tend to build their marriages on a foundation of romantic love only to find that when the flame dims, there is very little left in the marriage. Shipwrecked couples often struggle with companionate love because they have an impoverished understanding of what true friendship involves. They think it means having a buddy to hang out with. But true friendship has the power to separate a person from self-deceit and help him evolve into toward the person he one day hopes to become. As C. S. Lewis wrote in *The Four Loves*, "Friendship is—in a sense not at all derogatory to it—the least natural of all loves; the least instinctive. [Friendship] alone, of all the loves, seemed to raise you to the level of gods or angels."

This notion seems absurd if you consider a friend to be someone to hang out with, but Lewis's notion of friendship is a deep sharing of the self, a willingness to make sacrifices for the sake of another, even when it seems completely undesirable to do so. Lewis, a veteran of the First World War, understood friendship, in a very real way, as the willingness to take a bullet for someone else. Indeed, friendship, true companionate love, is best defined as the willingness to lay down your life for your friend.

Now, chances are, in the course of a marriage, a husband is not going to ask his wife to take a bullet for him. But he may ask her to do something almost as bad. He may ask her to watch football with him, go to a car show, or a million other things. Likewise, a wife may not ask her husband to throw himself on a grenade for her (unless she's *really* angry) but she may ask him to do something almost as bad. She may ask him to go shopping with her, or go to church, or a million other things. Your willingness to respond positively to those requests that run counter to your normal preferences is perhaps the best example of your ability to lay down your life, that is, exhibit both companionate and romantic love in a marriage.

Some people are well versed in both types of love, but most of us are more talented in one area than the other. For example, some people are capable of truly deep friendship. They can be counted on to be there no matter what, and they would willingly give you one of their major organs if you needed it. But many of these same people have a difficult time demonstrating the silly, playful, over-the-top behavior that the best kind of romantic love requires. In a similar vein, some people are all flash and no substance. They are good at sweeping you off your feet, but once you're up in the air, they don't know what to do with you—except maybe drop you on your ass.

Which are you better at, companionate or romantic love? Do you have a good balance in your marriage? Complete the following exercises to find out.

COMPANIONATE LOVE QUIZ

You and your spouse should take the following quiz separately. Do not add your scores together. The purpose of this quiz is to discover how strong each of you thinks your marital friendship is.

T F You have a hard time identifying what is important to your partner.

T F You think that some of the things that are important to your partner are silly, unreasonable, or beneath you.

T F You are not sure how you can be a part of helping your mate fulfill his or her dreams, goals, or values.

T F You are uncomfortable with how much your partner expects of you.

T F You feel love for your mate, but you are constantly being pulled away from him or her by other pressing matters.

T F Having your partner along is okay, but you really prefer doing the things you enjoy on your own or with your other friends.

T F Your partner discourages or belittles your input.

T F Your partner disregards you when you say he/she has hurt your feelings.

T F Your partner gives you the distinct impression that you are really not welcome to participate in his/her interests or activities. (He/she may not say it—but he/she doesn't have to.)

T F Your partner says he/she loves you, but seems to disregard your needs when making decisions, scheduling activities, or making plans.

Give yourself one point for each "T." The lower the score, the better.

- **0-2** Most likely you have a healthy amount of companionate love in your relationship.
- **3-5** Your companionate love is probably closer to 50-60 percent (instead of 70-80 percent).
  Talk about ways you and your mate will actively improve this. Be specific.
  Make a commitment to your plan.
- **6+** You need to do some *serious* work on your capacity to be friends to each other.
  Revisit chapter 3. If you find that discussing these issues with your mate is unproductive, you may wish to seek the help of a trusted pastor or counselor.

Remember, companionate love is defined as your desire and commit-ment to work for the good of your partner. It doesn't just apply to what you think you ought to do (that is, pay the bills or raise the kids); it really applies to the daily efforts you make to help your partner achieve the happiness and fulfillment that comes from pursuing the path he or she has mapped out.

Ideally, companionate love should contribute about 75 percent to the marital mix. To further assess the presence of companionate love in your marriage, answer and discuss the following questions with your partner.

How well do you love your mate?

Answer and discuss the following.

- List up to five things that you believe are most important to your mate.
- Describe the specific efforts you make on a daily basis to help your mate receive more fulfillment or enjoyment from the items you listed above.
- Do you enjoy involving your partner in the activities and ideas that excite you or are you a person who prefers people to stay out of your way?
- Do you work to develop an interest in the things that give your partner joy or are there some activities that you wish he or she would drop out of or at least stop talking to you about?

How well does your mate love you?

Answer and discuss the following.

- Does your partner actively solicit your opinions, encourage your growth, and work to further your interest and values? List specific examples.
- Does your partner look for ways to include you in activities and interests, or does he or she seem to view your involvement as a burden?
- In your opinion, does your mate make decisions with your needs in mind, plan with your interests in mind, and prepare his or her schedule with your importance in mind?

Share specific examples of each with your partner.

ROMANTIC LOVE QUIZ AND DISCUSSION

You and your spouse should each take the following quiz separately. Give yourself one point for each statement you mark "True" (T). Do not add your scores together. The purpose of this quiz is to discover how strong each of you thinks your romantic life is. If you "aren't sure," count it as a "False" (F) statement.

T   F   With my mate, I am generous both with my body and with displays of physical affection.

T   F   I am comfortable being playful and silly with my mate. I'm not afraid of making a little bit of a fool out of myself for love's sake.

T   F   Every day, I look for ways to show my mate how special he/she is to me.

T   F   I regularly express love for my mate verbally, physically, and through tokens of my affection.

T   F   I value our sexual relationship and seek out ways to keep it vital, fun, and satisfying.

T   F   My mate would agree that I make him/her feel special by my daily, loving efforts.

T   F   My mate would agree that I am a thoughtful, generous, and attentive sexual partner.

T   F   I could easily list five things I did this week to show my mate how important (s)he is to me.

T   F   When I feel like our relationship is losing some of its spark, I take the initiative to plan special surprises, dates, lovemaking, and other loving activities.

T   F   I actively look for ways to make my mate's life easier or more pleasant both when we are together and when we are apart.

Give yourself one point for each "T." The higher the score, the better.

- **8-10** Hubba Hubba. Romance is alive and well!
- **4-7**   You are probably giving average effort and getting an average return. Concentrate a little harder on how much your spouse and marriage mean to you and find ways to demonstrate that love more powerfully. Use the "Twenty-five Ways" list (page 90) as much as possible.

• 0-3   Wake up sleepy head! Don't wait until its too late to show your spouse how truly special (s)he is. If you don't, someone else might.

Finally, discuss these questions with your mate.

1. When do you feel most loved by your mate?
2. What do you appreciate most about being married to your mate?
3. In what ways would you like to be more loving to your mate? Does (s)he stop you?
4. What gestures of affection make you feel the most loved? What would you like to see more of from your mate?

4. Love Is the Means to Actualization

Exceptional couples know that love is the fuel that propels both their relationships and their identities toward actualization. When we love a person—that is, generously work for his or her good—we exercise most of the qualities we could ever wish to manifest in the course of our lives. Personal strength, generosity, patience, understanding, creativity, playfulness—all are qualities we exercise as we daily work for the good of our mate, that is, as we love them. Because the work that is love bears such good fruit not only in their relationships but in their own inner life, Exceptional couples work very hard to make love their first priority.

But this is easier said than done because we all struggle with selfishness, myself included. For all my high-minded talk about selfless loving, there is a big part of me that would rather do anything else. For the most part, I would much rather be comfortable, self-satisfying, and self-obsessed than I would be loving and giving. There are many days on which I cannot motivate myself to love simply because I know it is "the right thing to do." Many days when, if I am going to be loving, I need to find a more—shall we say—"selfish" reason to do it. Fortunately, I have one.

When I am too tired or too irritated to love as I know I should, I remind myself that when I choose not to love, I do not like the person I become. This is not just true for me, it is true of all human beings. To choose not to love is to reject our very humanness and turn ourselves into a grotesque caricature of what we were created to be.

Every day in my practice, I have the opportunity to witness the results of people choosing not to love. They all have their reasons, and for the most part I sympathize with those reasons. But the fact remains that the less a person exemplifies love in his life, the more he will become depressed, bitter, angry, estranged, paranoid, and confused. This is especially true in marriage. Shortly after deciding to go on a "love strike," a spouse begins to show signs of self-hate. Worse, it can easily get to the point where the spouse doesn't know how to find his way back to himself, much less to a satisfying relationship. Regardless of what husbands and wives in this situation eventually decide to do with their marriages, they must first work to reclaim their own dignity by responding to each other in more loving ways. A husband or wife may need to be more thoughtful, less defensive, more cooperative, more attentive, etc., not because their mate deserves it, but because they have a desperate need to reclaim their own dignity—to feel better about themselves.

The call to love is the human person's beginning, middle, and end. Those who respond to the call regardless of what their emotions have to say about it find fulfillment. Those who ignore the call find estrangement, loss, and isolation, first from others and then from themselves. The old saying is true: Happiness is not found in the pursuit of pleasure but in the attainment of virtue. Love, the privilege to work for the good of another, is the greatest virtue of all. To attain it is to find the greatest happiness.

The Power of Love

Charles was a client of mine who went through a crisis that helped raise his Conventional Star marriage to a Modern Partnership. Charles and his wife, Madeline, are a good example of both the work and reward inherent in Exceptional Loving.

Charles told me that he had always considered his marriage a happy one, but eight years into their relationship he started feeling estranged from his wife. He felt that Madeline was "too tired to be interested in my life, too tired to be interested in sex, and generally too busy to give much to the marriage." Initially Charles tried to change things by arguing with his wife over her perceived neglect. She told him that she was sorry, but that she was giving all that she had to give. In return, he pouted when Madeline was too tired to make love, and spent a great deal of time resenting how much he felt he was putting into the marriage.

I suggested to Charles that his relationship had reached a plateau and that it would not be able to progress unless he tried a daring experiment. He needed to be an example of the kind of attentive person he wanted Madeline to be. But he needed to do it for his own sake, without any guarantee that it would change anything in his marriage. He was willing to consider my suggestions, but had concerns about being taken advantage of. As he put it, "What if I do what you tell me and nothing changes, except now I'm killing myself to work on the marriage and she's happy being spoiled." I assured him that, after he had mastered the work I was describing, if he felt that his wife was not responding to his efforts, he might be justified in leaving the marriage. But I felt strongly that he had to do this for his own sake, and that either his marriage would improve, or he would be a better partner to a future spouse. He agreed to give it a try.

We started by making a list of all the things Madeline had asked Charles for over the years, like being a more active parent, becoming a more attentive listener, being less demanding, and several other requests. Charles's assignment was to do these things, whether he felt Madeline deserved his effort or not.

As Charles practiced his generosity, he began to become aware of his own selfishness. He noticed that, for each little thing he did, he not-quite-unconsciously expected some kind of payment from Madeline. He began realizing that this was a very limited kind of love, that not only was he holding back the best part of himself for fear of being taken advantage of, but he was also sending a continuous, implied message to Madeline that she "owed him." Putting himself in her place, he finally understood the possible cause of her holding back. As Charles told me, "I was trying to manipulate her into giving me the affection I wanted and then resenting her for refusing to be manipulated!"

With this awareness, Charles finally began to understand what I was asking him to do. He kept a close eye on his self-righteousness and made a point of doing his acts of love and service cheerfully. Likewise, he worked hard to compliment Madeline for the things he did appreciate in her, and he found that there were more than he expected.

About a month after this, Madeline came to him and told him that she had noticed that he had been different for a while. She wanted to thank him, but she also wanted to know what had motivated the change (up until this point he had not told her about his therapy). In session, Charles told me the conversation that followed was a turning point for their relationship. "We both ended up crying that night and apologizing to each other for taking our marriage for granted. That night we made a promise to each other to both try to give 100 percent."

A few years after our sessions concluded, I ran into Charles at the grocery store. He shook my hand and told me that he and Madeline were still going strong. "Sometimes it's been a struggle, but I never expected when I started all this that things could be as good as they are now. We share everything, we work together on everything, we make sure our marriage comes first." He glanced around and then added quietly, "And our sex life—all I can say is *wow!*"

From Charles's story, you can see that Exceptional Loving some-times involves both exceptional risks and exceptional work. But that's the nature of the animal. If you want your marriage to be all it can be to help you become all you wish to be, then you must be willing to give 100 percent all of the time, whether or not your spouse deserves it, whether or not you feel like it, because doing less is beneath your dignity as a human being.

6

Exceptional Service

The fruit of love is service.
—Mother Teresa

"The thing I love about Sean at this point in our lives is that he never waits for me to tell him what needs to be done around the house." Says Rita of her husband, "He wasn't always that way, but over the years he's made a real effort to be more attentive. The other day, I went to do some laundry and the basket was empty. He'd already taken care of it. That kind of thing happens all the time. It's probably the nicest way he shows how much he cares."

Romantic gestures, special time together, and tokens of affection are all direct and beautiful ways to express love to your mate, but it cannot end there. The fruitfulness, joy, and passion experienced by Exceptional couples are in many ways the result of their ability to express love through both the simple pleasures and mundane tasks of everyday life. It is this ability I call Exceptional Service.

How Do You Spell M-A-R-R-I-A-G-E?

The eight commandments that serve as the foundation for Exceptional Service are

M   Make sure to offer service, not servitude.
A   Activate both independent awareness and mutual commitment.
R   Relate requests to your marital imperative.
R   Relish opportunities to grow in competence.
I   Increase intimacy by sharing interests.
A   Avoid mind reading. Tell your mate what you need.
G   Go for similar competency, not "sameness."
E   Express love with your body and soul.

On the following pages, we'll take a brief look at each of these traits. As you read over them, I invite you to keep an eye open for ways you might exhibit greater service in your own marriage.

Make Sure to Offer Service, Not Servitude

The distinction between Exceptional Service and servitude (like the difference between sacrificial love and codependence you witnessed in the last chapter) hangs on the degree of personal strength present in the person who is doing the serving.

If I have very little personal strength, then any service I perform for you will be based on my fear that if I disappointed you in any way, you wouldn't like me anymore. This kind of service under the pain of rejection and loss defines mere servitude, and mere servitude has no place in any healthy marriage.

But if I have a great deal of personal strength, I will perform acts of service not because I am afraid of losing your favor but rather because I place a high value on love, and I know that if I love you I must work for your good. Under these conditions, the service I give benefits not only you but me as well, because the more I serve, the more loving I become, and the more loving I become, the more congruent I am with both my identity and my marital imperative. When service is performed in a context of personal strength and performed with the intention of nurturing and supporting another, rather than performed to prevent losing another's favor, then it can be called Exceptional Service.

Activate Independent Awareness and Mutual Commitment

The Exceptional husband and wife are both independently aware of the various emotional, relational, and domestic tasks required for maintaining their marriage and home, and they are mutually committed to attending to these tasks. Exceptional spouses do not sit around waiting for an invitation to serve. They make themselves aware of the jobs that need to be done (shopping, cleaning, yard work, planning "couple time," maintaining the social calendar, etc.) and they seek out opportunities to do them—eagerly and cheerfully.

Relate Requests to Your Marital Imperative

In the chapter on Exceptional Fidelity, you discovered the advantages of weighing others' requests against your marital imperative as opposed to merely your emotional reactions.

In a similar way, an Exceptional spouse does not base his or her response to a mate's request for a particular service on emotions or comfort level, but on the following question: "Will performing this service (or learning this skill) help me grow in the values, goals, or ideals that are important to me or our marital imperative?"

If the answer is yes, then the Exceptional spouse is obliged—not to his or her mate, but to him or herself—to fulfill the request. Emotions, comfort, or skill level may justifiably vary the speed with which some requests are granted, but if the request is consistent with the marital imperative, the Exceptional spouse must be willing to at least begin the process of complying with the request. To do less is to be less than true to one's self and this is a recipe for poor self-esteem.

If, on the other hand, the answer is no, then the Exceptional spouse will be able to refuse the request on solid grounds, unless or until the mate can demonstrate that granting the request would be consistent with their marital imperative to grant the request. Honestly, it is rare that a request by a spouse falls outside a marital imperative, but a couple may legitimately argue a particular point. For example, you may recall Todd and Sherry from chapter 4. Sherry believed that by counseling her friend, Angela, she was being compassionate, and so, was behaving appropriately when she left Todd night after night. Only after Todd was able to appeal to the quality of "togetherness" that they had listed on their marital imperative was he able to convince her that, noble as her intentions were, her priorities were somewhat askew.

Relying on your marital imperative as your guide for whether to respond positively or negatively to a request by your mate decreases nagging, whining, or obnoxious bargaining in a marriage. Since your yes is yes and your no is no and both are based on solid ground, there is no room for emotionally manipulative techniques like "trying to guilt" someone into doing something (or for that matter "feeling guilted" into doing it). There is room for intelligent discussion and respectful disagreement, but never manipulative nonsense.

Relish Opportunities to Grow in Competence

Exceptional Service challenges a person to reach beyond his or her present limitations and develop greater competencies. It is Exceptional Service more than anything else that explains the dance of competence—the seemingly effortless way Exceptional couples accomplish the tasks of daily living and loving.

To give Exceptional Service to your mate is to constantly challenge yourself. You must be willing to address your shortcomings, learn new skills, and gain new strengths. Couples in still-good, but less-than-Exceptional relationships tend to view marriage as an institution which provides shelter from their shortcomings. To varying degrees, Deadly, Shipwrecked, and Conventional husbands and wives don't do certain relationship or domestic tasks because "I'm not good at it" or "I don't like to do it." Or they say, "Thank God I'm married because that means I don't ever have to cook/earn a living/be romantic/pump my own gas/clean the house ever again." This logic is superficially appealing, but the more a couple uses excuses like these, the more that couple tends to feel powerless and estranged in their marriage. Why? Because either they must resort to nagging and cajoling to get their mate to do certain things for them (or experience nagging and cajoling themselves), or they are forced to throw up their hands in hopeless disgust that they will ever get their needs met. An attitude of Exceptional Service cuts through all of this by allowing husbands and wives to relish every opportunity to do the work true love requires and practice their dance of competence.

Increase Intimacy by Sharing Interests

We'll examine this factor more closely in chapter 10, but as Exceptional Service motivates you and your mate to become both more interested and more competent in each other's worlds, you open the door to greater intimacy. Think about it, whom do you count as your closest friends? Probably those people who do the things you do, are concerned with similar issues as yourself, and enjoy many of the things that you enjoy. In short, you are best friends with the people who are competent in more or less the same areas as yourself. Now, think of those marriages where the husband and wife get along well enough, but don't consider each other best friends. You will probably note that the husband and wife not only have separate household responsibilities but also have a great number of interests they enjoy separately with separate sets of friends ("You know how much I hate doing X. Why don't you ask so and so to go with you?"). These couples may even tend to think very differently than one another about important issues that touch on both of them, which is why they may confide to their same-sex friends, "I love my husband/wife, but you know how men/women are." In such marriages, the husbands and wives have dissimilar areas of competence. Note, I am not saying that these couple's marriages are bad or undesirable—in fact, they may be very satisfactory to the couple—I am simply saying they are not getting from their marriage what they could, and often, they know it. What they may not know is that the reason they are not getting all they could from their marriages is that both the husband and wife are unwilling to push themselves beyond the comfortable boundaries of their specific areas of competence. This is the root of that pandemic marital problem known as "growing apart." Exceptional Service is the only cure for this problem. By developing a heart for Exceptional Service, the couple draws their two worlds together. While they do not "lose themselves" in each other, they become familiar with every nook and cranny of their mate's soul.

Avoid Mind Reading: Tell Your Mate What You Need

I would be horrified to think that someone would read this chapter and think that Exceptional couples somehow "just know" each other's needs and magically fulfill them. This idea represents the dance of insipid romantic fantasy more than it does the dance of competence.

While it is a lovely thing when a husband and wife anticipate each other's needs, most Exceptional Service begins *after* a partner makes his or her needs public. Exceptional Service is not clairvoyance. It is the willingness to act positively and with dignity when your mate asks for more than you may have been hoping to give. Exceptional husbands and wives are willing, but they still must be asked.

Go for Similar Competency, Not Sameness

A second misconception I hope to avoid is giving the impression that Exceptional couples must like all the same things, do all the same things, and think in exactly the same ways. This is impossible. Exceptional husbands and wives are not "the same." They simply strive to be similarly competent. An Exceptional husband may be a God-and-country conservative and his Exceptional wife a bleeding-heart liberal, but if they are both politically astute, they share a level of competence which will contribute to increased intimacy. Jack Sprat may eat no fat, his wife may eat no lean, but as long as they are both competent chefs, they'll have something interesting to debate about, and the more they debate, the more they will learn about themselves and each other. And the more capable they will be of loving and serving each other well. Sameness, in and of itself, does not build intimacy. Shared competency does.

Express Love With Your Body and Soul

Through Exceptional Service, a couple gives two gifts to each other: the gift of the body and the gift of the soul.

The gift of the body is the freely offered gift of one's physical labor for the good of one's mate and one's home. You might note that there is a sexual undertone to this phrase. This is intentional. Though the sexual aspects of the gift of the body (and for that matter the gift of the soul) will be explored in depth in chapter 11, it is fitting that the sexual undercurrents be present in the context of domestic service as well. Why? Because how good a person is at physically working for the good of one's mate and one's home is manifested in the couple's sexual relationship. It is a marital cliche to say that sex begins in the kitchen, but it is true nevertheless. The source of the sexual passion in Exceptional Marriages is the passionate Exceptional Service those couples render to each other in every arena. It is for this reason that some philosophers refer to domestic service as "social intercourse," the intimacy created through daily service and communication. When an Exceptional Couple makes love, they celebrate how well they respond to one another's needs in and outside the bedroom.

The gift of the soul refers to those acts of service that support your mate's mental, emotional, and spiritual well-being. For example, in an argument, is your first goal mutual understanding or is it proving how right you are? Are you a good listener? Do you follow through on promises? Are you good at expressing your mate's specialness? Are you complimentary of your mate on a consistent basis? Are you grateful for your mate? Do you tell him or her? All of these are examples of the gift of the soul: the way you communicate your love, one spirit to another.

Practicing the eight attitudes of Exceptional Service in your marriage allows you and your mate to suck the marrow out of every aspect of your life together no matter how simple or common. Too often, couples think of love as something that is separate from the daily life of the marriage. Romance is saved for date nights, affection is only expressed in cards and flowers. While I would be the last person to undermine the utmost importance of such gestures, they cannot replace the somewhat more humble, but in many ways more meaningful, expressions of love: doing outdoor work that isn't specifically yours to do, folding the laundry when it wasn't "your turn," jumping up to wash the dishes without being asked, taking the kids out for a night so your spouse can get some quiet time, learning to share in one of your mate's hobbies though it really isn't "your thing." These, and a multitude of other simple acts, are all ways a lover makes a gift of his or her very self. And there is no gift more precious.

Exceptional Service in Action: Three Couples

Each of the following couples represents a different way Exceptional Service manifests itself in the life of a marriage. It is my hope that their stories will inspire you to think of the simple opportunities you might be missing to fulfill the promise you made at the end of chapter 3: to be the influence that helps your mate become the most complete, contented, and fulfilled person he or she can be, even when doing so challenges you or makes you uncomfortable.

Clarissa and Joe

"I've always hated professional sports" says Clarissa, who has been married to Joe for fifteen years. "I don't mean I just didn't like it, I hated it. I honestly thought it was responsible for much of what is wrong in the world. I saw it as the glorification of a bunch of high-paid spoiled brats combined with the excesses of corporate greed all coming together to take advantage of all too forgiving fans with wallets in hand."

"Unfortunately I married a guy who would watch ESPN if they were showing 'Extreme Peanut Farming.' Needless to say, this has led to a few fights between Joe and me. To be fair, he's always tried to be reasonable about it. He probably hasn't watched half as much as he wanted to, but I just couldn't get past wanting him to stop all together. I resented the time he spent at games or in front of the television. I wanted him to be with me, doing something I liked.

"I have this one friend who I'm really close to, and I used to always complain to her about this thing with Joe. But I think she was getting fed up with me because one day she stopped her usual shoulder-to-cry-on routine and said, 'Clare, I don't know what to tell you. I don't think its fair for you to ask him to totally give this up, and you're making yourself crazy. For your own sake, you've either got to dump him, join him, or be happy with things the way they are.'

"Of course I couldn't leave him. Despite this one thing we really did have a great marriage. But I couldn't just leave things the way they were because I just wasn't happy. I missed him. I mean, its not like I just sat there sighing, watching the clock and waiting for the game to be done or anything. I had plenty to do, and plenty of friends I could do it with, and I did. I just missed him. That left one thing, joining him.

"My first thought was 'no way!' but then I thought to myself, 'Who did I think I was?' I mean, what kind of person was I being? Not only was I demeaning something that obviously meant a great deal to Joe, but I was placing really unfair demands on him. I never thought of myself as controlling, but I realized that was exactly what I was being, or trying to be. I still had my hang-ups about sports, but I realized they were my hang-ups. And it wasn't as if my boycott was doing any good. The game went on. The only thing I was doing was putting distance between myself and Joe. I decided to join him. I figured if nothing else it would make me more well-rounded. But I didn't want him to make a big deal about it, I wanted it to be a surprise. I took out a couple of books from the library on the basic rules of football and baseball, Joe's favorites, and I started paying attention to the sports reports on the evening news.

"One day there was a football game that I knew he really wanted to see. Before he had the chance to say anything I asked him if 'we' were going to watch the game today. At first he thought I was being sarcastic and started to get a little defensive. But I told him that I was tired of being a sports widow and I wanted to see what all the fuss was about. He was still pretty suspicious, but we watched the game together that night. To be honest, I was pretty bored. But I tried to join in as best I could and I think I impressed him that I knew anything at all about the game. Regardless, after it was over, he told me he really appreciated what I did for him. He said it was even better than making him my Bailey's Irish Cheesecake. That's pretty high praise coming from Joe.

"I still probably wouldn't count sports as among my top ten favorite things, but I have to admit, it's not so bad. We make popcorn, throw it at the screen when there's a bad play. And throw it at each other just to be silly. One time, we were having such a good time with each other, we started making out and missed the rest of the game! That doesn't happen nearly as much as I would like, but it wouldn't happen at all if I didn't push myself a little bit to be there. I'm glad to be able to participate in something he enjoys so much. It's nice to know what he's talking about when he starts reciting statistics. And he seems to enjoy sharing that stuff with me. My sports questions are still pretty basic, but he's happy to answer them. It's brought us closer together. He isn't afraid of my reaction anymore when he talks about sports or says he wants to catch a game, and it's made him try harder to do things that he knows I like. I was shocked one weekend when he told me he planned on blowing off a game and taking me to the community arts and crafts festival. He—jokingly—said that if I could learn to live with football, he could put up with 'learning 101 uses for dryer lint' (of course, I had to punch him).

"We're trying harder with each other. I really feel good about that, and we feel great about each other."

Some of you may be wondering, "Why did Clarissa have to change? Shouldn't Joe have given up football for the sake of the marriage?" The fact is, it could have worked out this way, and if it did, that would be perfectly fine. The problem, in this case, is that Joe was not the one with the unmet need. Joe enjoyed Clarissa's company very much, but he was happy to let her have what he considered to be "her space" while he watched a game. Spending this specific time together was Clarissa's need, and so it was her responsibility to do what she had to do to meet her need.

Let me try to illustrate my point this way. Imagine that we are together, and I am so hungry that I can't possibly wait another minute to eat. You, on the other hand, couldn't be less hungry. That leaves me two choices, I can sit around, huffing and puffing, and wait for you to get hungry and make us both a meal, or I could fix myself something to eat. Of the two possibilities, the only healthy choice I can make is to accept responsibility for my need and meet it, regardless of what other alternative I might prefer. I could sit around whining about how "If you loved me you would cook something for me right now." But that would be pathetic beyond words. It is my hunger, not yours. In the same way, Clarissa's hunger to share some specific time with Joe was her need and her responsibility. By performing her Exceptional Service (that is, learning about sports) she was empowered to meet her need, increase her competence, and achieve greater intimacy in her marriage.

Ellie and Mark

Ellie and Mark had been married for twenty-three years. Mark had always had a hard time expressing his emotions. He tried to show Ellie his love by "being there" for her and working hard. As much as she appreciated him for what he did do, she sometimes complained of feeling "all alone" because Mark wasn't much of a talker. Additionally, Mark was very backward about even simple public displays of affection and he didn't say "I love you" nearly as often as Ellie wanted to hear it.

"I thought she'd get over it. I figured she knew I loved her. But one day I came home and found her crying. She didn't want to tell me what was wrong at first, but finally she said she had been talking with a friend who had just gotten back from her second honeymoon. Her friend had talked about how romantic her husband had been. Ellie said she was ashamed to admit it to me, but she was jealous. She said there were lots of times where she just wanted me to hold her, but she knew how uncomfortable I was and so she just stayed quiet.

"My family was never real touchy-feely, if you know what I mean. My dad was always working and my mom was a real proper Presbyterian lady. I knew they loved me, they just weren't showy about it. I never thought much about being showy with my affection for Ellie because I never figured it was very important—it certainly wasn't very important to me. But when I came home that day and saw her crying there, I knew I had to do something. When I was gone, I didn't want to be remembered as a 'stuffed shirt' like my teenage daughter sometimes called me, and I needed Ellie to know how much I really did love her.

"Shortly after that, Ellie and I were out at the mall. I remember she was looking at a sales rack when I thought to myself, 'You should be holding her hand.' I'll tell you, I just didn't want to do it. I felt like some silly teenager—I was just as embarrassed. But I figured it wouldn't kill me to do something that obviously meant so much to her. I might feel like I was dying of embarrassment, but I guess I wouldn't really. Finally, I said under my breath, 'Ellie, would you mind if I held your hand?'

"And wouldn't you know it? She just kept right on looking at the rack. She didn't hear me. I almost took it as a sign from God not to do it again, but, well, I figure I'd come this far. So I asked her again.

"You could have knocked her over with a feather. She didn't say a word—which is pretty unusual for her. She just smiled, took my hand, and we walked together like that for most of that day. I even made a point of sitting on the same side of the booth as her when we had lunch in the restaurant later. I had a lot of strange feelings about it. I felt happy to be doing something for her and it did feel good to be affectionate with the girl I loved. But at the same time, I kept feeling like I was doing something, like I wasn't acting my age. I still have a lot of work to do, but I try to push myself a little bit more every day. If I can help it, I don't ever want to be the source of her tears again."

Both of the couples you've read about so far illustrate that the essence of Exceptional Service is a willingness to put yourself out for your mate emotionally, relationally, and temporally. Giving Exceptional Service means anticipating and responding to your spouse's needs whether or not those needs make a whole lot of sense to you. Through this willingness, an individual spouse's competence increases, which gives him more to share with his mate, which in turn builds intimacy in the marriage. Even though the examples I have given so far describe more of what I call service of the soul (that is, doing things to attend to the emotional, and mental well-being of one's mate), the more obvious type of service, service of the body (that is, doing the physical labor necessary to maintain a comfortable home) has a similar positive effect on both competence and intimacy.

Arianna and Peter

Arianna and Peter have been married for twelve years. Here, they describe how letting go of domestic scorekeeping and practicing Exceptional Service in their home helped draw them closer together.

PETER: Arianna and I both work, so there never seems to be enough time to get everything done. Add our two kids to the mix and it makes for a pretty busy life.

ARIANNA: It's important to both of us to be on top of things but we could never agree on who should do what, when. We tried to set up a list of chores, some for Peter, some for me, some for the kids, but everybody would end up putting everything off and eventually either the chores wouldn't be done or I'd have to waste my weekend doing them.

PETER: I tried to help, but I think that was part of the problem. I thought of doing things to maintain the house as "helping Arianna." It just never occurred to me that we were both responsible for getting things done.

ARIANNA: Yeah. For the most part, unless I specifically told Peter to do something, he wouldn't think to do it. He was good at doing the outside jobs, mowing the lawn, cleaning gutters—you know, things you think of as "typical guy jobs," but when it came to the inside housework, it seemed like that was supposed to be my domain. The funny thing was, we weren't a traditional family. Peter and I didn't split up any other area of our lives that way. We just seemed to fall into it. I really resented it.

It started to change when Peter and I sat down to do our marital imperative. One of the qualities we identified as being important to us was "cooperation." When we talked about what we would need to do to have a more cooperative marriage I suggested we look at our housekeeping. We decided to make a list of all the regular maintenance we had to do—indoor and outdoor. We'd done this before—but this time, instead of splitting up the chores, we decided to take a "see it, do it" attitude. The goal was not to wait around for anyone to tell anyone else what to do. We were both to be aware of all the things that needed to be done and do them whenever we had the time.

PETER: We even got the kids involved. They had been a little lazy too, stepping over things instead of putting them away and so on. We decided that we were going to exhibit more cooperation as an entire family. It was tough at first. I had a little bit harder time mentally keeping up with all the chores. Sometimes I was tired and it was just easier to forget. But one day I came home to find Arianna up on a ladder cleaning out the front gutters. She'd always left that to me before. I had a major attack of "the guilts" I tried to talk her down off the roof but she said, "Its okay. I had some time so I thought why should I leave it to you?" That's when I knew I'd better get serious.

Eventually we got to the point where we were both aware of what needed to be done and were both on top of doing it. Like I said, initially it was hard for me, but I got to thinking, If I lived by myself I'd have to keep up with all this stuff anyway, why should being married make me less competent?

ARIANNA: Besides, it was having a really positive impact on our marriage. We cut way back on the "Who's turn is it to do such and such" fights. Plus, it was fun working side by side.

PETER: It reminded me of how well we worked together when we were having the house built. We did some of the work ourselves, and we worked side by side on the painting and trim work. We really connected then. This was another opportunity to do that.

Through their conscientious efforts, Peter and Arianna learned the steps to the dance of competence, the graceful way Exceptional couples accomplish the tasks of daily living and loving. Granted, the dance of competence requires a great deal of effort, but like all masters, Exceptional couples make their art look easy. What enables the work to get done so smoothly in Exceptional couples' homes is exactly what Peter and Arianna described: They don't sit around waiting to be told what to do or keep score over who's doing what. They don't have to, because both husband and wife are acutely aware of the things that need to be done, and they are both equally committed to doing the work. Of course, they may have lapses now and then; after all, you can't be "on duty" all of the time. But these lapses are the exception, not the rule, and so they are fairly easy to forgive—and redirect as necessary.

Think of marriage as a garden. Just like weeding a garden promotes the growth of all the plants in it, Exceptional Service promotes the growth of intimacy by weeding out the dependency that could otherwise choke it off. The following will help you more effectively tend your own garden.

How's the Service?

It has been my hope, throughout this chapter, to convince you of the merits of a very countercultural idea: Exceptional Service. If you would like to examine your relationship for additional opportunities to enhance intimacy through service, take a few minutes to do the exercise that follows. Because the gift of the soul is a fairly large category that encompasses communication, gratitude, playfulness, and good humor in a marriage, I have decided to examine these topics more closely in subsequent chapters. For now, I would like you to concentrate on building greater intimacy by learning the steps to the dance of competence. Specifically, I am going to ask you to consider the areas of your relationship and home life where you and your mate have dissimilar competencies, with the intention of drawing those separate worlds closer together. By doing this, you increase your own efficiency, decrease the chances of growing apart, and begin to unleash the true intimate potential of your marriage.

Part One: Examining Your Spheres of Influence

You and your mate probably have areas in your marriage where one of you is more competent than the other. These represent your spheres of influence—those areas in which one of you exercises more control than the other. These areas could be opportunities for you and your mate to draw closer together through Exceptional Service.

On a scale of 1-10 (1 is not at all competent, 10 is extremely competent), rate your own and your mate's competency in the following spheres of influence.

Sphere 1: Finances
Includes: earning, spending, planning, and saving.
Husband ____   Wife ____

Sphere 2: Domestic Responsibilities
Includes: cleaning the home, cooking the meals, shopping, etc.
Husband ____   Wife ____

Sphere 3: Home Improvements
Includes: improving the appearance of the home, doing construction and landscaping projects, or heavier maintenance.
Husband ___ Wife ___

Sphere 3: Social Planning
Includes: planning family and couple time, outings with friends, community involvements, and get-togethers with families of origin.
Husband ___ Wife ___

Sphere 4: Other Areas
You may apply this to any or all of the following areas: parenting, sexual relationship, spiritual/religious involvement, or any other area which you would like to examine more closely.

Write identified area here: _____
Husband ___ Wife___

After reviewing your scores in the previous section, discuss the following questions.

a. How would your relationship benefit by a greater sharing in these areas?
b. What could the less competent mate do to increase his or her competence in these areas?
c. What could both spouses do to contribute more to these areas?
d. What obstacles do you foresee getting in the way of a greater partnership in these areas?
e. How could you overcome these obstacles?

Part Two: Maintaining Awareness

One of the biggest difficulties in learning the dance of competence, at least as far as it relates to domestic chores, is remembering all the steps (that is, maintaining your awareness of all that has to be done and how often). The chart on page 116 is an example of a Home Planner that can help you and your mate—and even your kids—develop that "see it, do it" attitude which exemplifies the dance of competence. Feel free to develop your own version, and be sure to post it in several prominent places (but resist the temptation to staple it to your mate's head).

The Weekly Home Planner

To practice love through Exceptional Service, we are making a commitment to be aware of, and attentive to, the following:

Daily Jobs

Weekly Jobs

Special Needs for This Week

Ways to Make This Week Special for Each Other

Not every couple needs something like this to help them stay on top of the things that must be done. Use it, or your own version of it, if you find it to be helpful.

At this point, you probably have a better understanding of something I wrote in the last chapter: that Exceptional couples do not view marriage as a labor of love, so much as they view love as the labor of marriage. Exceptional Service is why. I love my wife very deeply and, generally speaking, I am fairly good with words. But sometimes when I try to tell her how important she is to me, I can't find the right words. They all seem insufficient in some way. While I do not always succeed, I try to use Exceptional Service to speak the kind of love to my wife for which there are no words. I would invite you to do the same to the best of your ability.

Let service be the fruit of your love.

7

Exceptional Rapport

I have spent most of my life studying women,
and I still have no idea what they want.

—ATTRIBUTED TO SIGMUND FREUD

MANY THINK that the gulf separating men from women is so wide, it's
a wonder that we ever got together in the first place. According to
these people, when it comes to relationships, women are warm,
nurturing, loving, attentive, romantic, good listeners, thoughtful, and
cooperative.

Men, on the other hand, like football.

There is even some good research to back up these popular
assumptions. Deborah Tannen's work on the many differences between male and female communication patterns presents a great deal
of food for thought (see her book, *You Just Don't Understand*).
Likewise, the popular author John Gray has built an empire observing
and exploiting the basic differences between men and women in his
Mars and Venus books.

But before anyone accuses me of having a bad case of Venus envy,
I'd like to point out that while it is easy to assume the truth about
gender stereotypes—for example, that men prefer sexual displays of

affection while women tend to be more emotional and romantic, and that, in conflict, men retreat into a cave and women become more verbal—some studies have found that these characteristics, and others like them, are actually reversed in at least 20 percent of men and women. This is an important statistic for two reasons. First, it tells us that something beyond gender differences is responsible for a significant amount of miscommunication between husbands and wives. Second, upon finishing one of the more popular relationship books, many of us think that we have it all figured out: Wives will do X for their men, husbands will do Y for their women, and everyone will live happily ever after. But a large number of husbands and wives simply don't fit the mold. Further, while it is well established that some men and women exhibit remarkable differences in their capacities for emotional and linguistic expression, it is indisputably true that men and women in Exceptional marriages do not exhibit those differences. As Dr. Gottman reports in his widely respected book, *Why Marriages Succeed or Fail,* "we find that, by and large, in happy marriages there are no gender differences in emotional expression. But in unhappy marriages, all the gender differences… emerge."

This coincides with my observation (see chapter 2) that Shipwrecked couples experience the greatest amount of estrangement between men and women, Conventional/Apprenticeship couples experience considerably fewer problems related to gender differences, and for Exceptional couples, the issue is essentially null and void. All of this allows me to assert that while husbands and wives in less-than-exceptional marriages may be from Mars and Venus respectively, Exceptional husbands and wives are both native to planet Earth.

How Do They Do It?

Exceptional Rapport is the skill that allows Exceptional husbands and wives to become emotional and communicative peers, and it is one aspect of the service of the soul we discussed in the last chapter. In essence, Exceptional Rapport is Exceptional Service as applied to communication and emotional expression. Exceptional Rapport is achieved in two stages:

a. Understanding the common humanity that unites women and men

b. Understanding and becoming fluent in all the "love languages," those unique ways individuals prefer to give and receive love

In the following pages, we will examine each more closely.

Understanding Common Humanity

Boys and girls do start out differently. They have different experiences and different physiology. But, sociologically speaking, as boys and girls grow and mature, they tend to fall into one of two categories. Let's call the first category the "same-gender friendship group." In this category, young men have mostly male friends while young women have mostly female friends, and each group tends not to think of the other except as potential romantic/sexual partners. People in this category tend to agree with Billy Crystal's character in the movie *When Harry Met Sally* when he says that "men and women can't be friends" because of the sexual tension. These men and women tend to learn the rules of courting each other, but not the different set of rules which enable them to befriend each other.

Now, let's call the second category the "mixed-gender friendship group." Young men and women in this group associate freely with each other, counting many members of the opposite sex as platonic friends. Of course, there is some degree of sexual tension here, but for the most part, this is secondary to the development of healthy friendships with a variety of people that includes members of the opposite sex.

When men and women raised in same-gender friendship groups grow up and marry, they tend to be at a disadvantage. Because so much of their time was spent with same-gender friends, their socialization process is not yet complete, and much about the way the opposite sex views the world remains a mystery. Men and women raised in same-gender friendship groups tend to cling to those stereotypes which have been validated by their own limited experience, but would have naturally fallen away had they simply been better socialized. The basic lesson learned from participation in same-gender friendship groups is, "Men are men because they *do* A and express themselves B, and women are women because they *do* X and express themselves Y—and never the twain shall meet." As such, marital therapy for couples in this category tends not to address marital problems per se so much as it attempts to teach remedial social skills to both the husband and wife, who, due to a lack of experience, never learned the rules governing effective cross-gender communication.

Conversely, men and women who grew up in mixed-gender friendship groups tend to have more advanced social, emotional, and communicative skills. Because they have engaged in varied, daily, casual interactions with one another, both young men and women in the mixed-gender groups learn each other's rules for dealing with problems, sharing emotions, and building friendships. Eventually, men and women in this category incorporate each other's successful communication strategies and discard the less successful ones. Through trial and error, they develop a more or less shared set of social and communicative rules which allows rapport between males and females in the group to flourish.

I would also suggest that young men and women who participate in mixed-gender friendship groups may exhibit a greater capacity for Exceptional Service. You will remember in the last chapter that I defined Exceptional Service as the willingness to push past one's immediate skills and comfort level to meet the needs of one's mate. From a fairly early age, young men and women in mixed-gender friendship groups are required to do just this. In these groups, if people are going to be able to understand each other, young men must move beyond their basic "guy" ways of doing things and young women must move beyond their basic "girl" ways of doing things. In the process, they learn that relationships based on true friendship require a willingness to be stretched. The payoff, of course, is that those who are willing to stretch become more fully integrated human beings. Men and women raised in mixed-gender friendship groups believe that the saying, "Men are men because they *do* X and express themselves Y, and women are women because they *do* A and express themselves B" ignores a greater truth. Specifically, that both men and women were created with the capacity for love, warmth, understanding, compassion, communication, rationality, affection, and all the qualities that are essential for a happy marriage. And because both men and women are created with this capacity, in order to be true to themselves, they must exhibit and exercise these qualities to their fullest potential. In this way, masculinity and femininity are not foreign languages spoken by Martians and Venusians as they awkwardly try hook up at the Interplanetary High School dance. Rather, masculinity and femininity become the prisms through which men and women express a shared humanity.

Negotiating the basic differences between men and women is the first step to achieving Exceptional Rapport, but negotiating these differences is far beyond the scope of this book. The subject has been examined in depth by others, specifically, Gary Smalley in *Hidden Keys to a Loving Lasting Marriage,* John Gray in his Mars and Venus series, and Deborah Tannen in *You Just Don't Understand* and others. I must refer you to them if you require some remedial help overcoming the basic estrangement between men and women. But for those couples who have advanced beyond the Mars and Venus stage, and were wondering "What's next?" the remainder of this chapter will examine the second step in achieving Exceptional Rapport: becoming fluent in all the "love languages."

Love Languages

What I am calling "love languages" were originally identified by linguist John Grinder and mathematician Richard Bandler.*

There are three major love languages, three basic ways people prefer to give and receive love. An individual's primary love language is determined by the sense (sight, sound, touch) which is most highly developed in that person. So, for example, if your visual sense is most highly developed you will prefer a more visual love language. As a result you will prefer to show your mate how much you love her by giving her cards, flowers, small gifts, love notes, well-presented meals with candlelight, and so on. For you, to feel close to someone, you have to be able to see their love ("Don't just tell me you love me, *show* me!"). Of all the ways your mate could demonstrate affection for you, you prefer the things you can look at. Likewise, when you are "in the mood," romantic lighting, lingerie, atmosphere may be almost as important as the act of lovemaking itself.

Alternatively, if your sense of hearing is most highly developed, you will have a more auditory love language. You will probably be given to saying "I love you" 500,000 times per day, having extended con-

---

*While Bandler and Grinder were not initially concerned with analyzing romantic relationships (they were interested in studying and codifying effective communication patterns and general rapport building strategies), their work was later applied to relationships by others, most notably, marital therapist Leslie Cameron-Bandler in her book *Solutions.*

versations about absolutely anything, calling your mate silly pet names in a playful voice, singing love songs—all the things you could possibly invent to tell your mate how special she is to you. As a person who primarily uses an auditory love language, in order to feel close to someone, you need to be communicating with them. An unstated rule you live by is "if they ain't talking, they ain't lovin'." Likewise, an important part of lovemaking may be saying how good your mate is making you feel and hearing your mate tell you how good you are making him or her feel. In the throws of passion, the more you talk, the louder you talk (and perhaps the more randy that talk is), the better it is. And you want to be loved the same way.

Finally, if your sense of touch is most highly developed, you will exhibit a more kinesthetic love language. You will value "just being together." For you, an afternoon spent working side by side without saying a word, or cuddling on the couch, or similar ways of "getting in touch" with one another will be sheer bliss. When you make love, you don't want to be distracted by all those "props" (lingerie, candlelight) that visual people like or all that talking that auditory people prefer. You would prefer to feel your way around your mate, doing what comes naturally, and getting to the "good stuff" as soon as possible. And you want your mate to love you the same way.

Applying these sensory-based languages to relationships is a fairly new concept, but the field of educational psychology has extensively validated the idea of sensory-based communication styles. To best explain what I mean, I need to take you back to grade school for a minute. Kids all learn differently and teachers spend a great deal of time trying to figure out their students' learning styles. For example, children who learn better by reading and taking notes are said to have a visual learning style. Students who learn best through lectures, songs, and being "talked through" tasks have an auditory learning style. Finally, kids who learn best by doing hands-on projects and activities have a kinesthetic learning style. These styles can change over time, but they never go away completely because they are neurologically based. That is, they are dependent upon the senses which are most highly developed in a particular student. When we become adults, our learning styles don't go away, they become our communication styles, or, for our purposes, the love language in which we are most fluent.

"Wait a minute," some of you are thinking, "there are five senses. If love languages are really based on the senses, wouldn't there be five of them as well?" The short answer to this is that I suppose that you could find a way to smell how much you love your mate, but frankly, I don't want to know about it.

A more serious answer is that yes, there are five sensory languages (Bandler and Grinder called them "modalities"), but most people's senses of sight, sound, and touch are more highly developed (and more practical) than their senses of taste or smell, and so those senses make up the three primary love languages. For most of us, the olfactory/gustatory love language is—at best—a distant second language. Because this is a fairly rare "dialect," I will not deal with it here. (However, if you want a good illustration of the olfactory/gustatory love language, pick up Isabel Allende's book *Aphrodite: A Memoir of the Senses,* a kind of cookbook-relationship book all in one. To give one example, in an interview on public radio WHYY's program *Fresh Air,* Allende said that when she and her husband have a fight, she will sometimes make a strong-smelling mushroom soup. When her husband smells the simmering soup, he knows it is her signal to come to her from wherever he is because she is ready to make up.)

To see which of the three major love languages you and your mate speak most fluently, complete the following exercise.

Love Language Exercise

Chances are you use all of your five senses, but you will favor one or two of them when it comes to giving and receiving love. The following are some of the most prominent characteristics, speech patterns, and preferences associated with each love language. Write "M" (me) next to each statement that you would agree with. Write "P" (partner) next to each quality that your mate would agree with. You will probably mark some in each category. You are looking for the category you mark the most items in. This will be your primary love language.

THE VISUAL (SEEING) LOVE LANGUAGE

___ "*Show* me that you love me."

___ Flowers, love notes, cards most meaningful (not just liked).

___ "Presentation" is very important (that is, presents wrapped nicely, meals arranged decoratively on a well-set table)—think, Martha Stewart.

__ Lighting is essential to mood.

__ I'm turned on by visual stimuli (for example, lingerie that looks sexy even though it may be ungodly uncomfortable).

__ Clothes are important. Looking good is more important than comfort or practicality.

__ My desktops and visible surfaces are as neat as a pin. My desk drawers and closets, however, are a disaster. Out of sight, out of mind.

__ I am always making plans and am productive. I can track 100 projects at once.

__ I am good at decorating or other visual arts (photography, painting).

__ I make neat piles out of everything you put in front of me.

__ I tend to clean and tidy up when stressed.

__ I daydream often.

__ I speak quickly and use a lot of words.

__ I tend to be uptight/proper/detail oriented.

__ I enjoy books with vivid descriptions/pictures.

__ I love to keep journals, makes plans, and write lists.

__ Charts, graphs, or other visual aids are very helpful to me. I learn by watching.

__ I use lots of visual metaphors in speech, such as, "see my point," "I've got to focus," "imagine that," "it seems vague," "it seems clear," "I can see right through you," "I'm seeing things in a new light," "I'm drawing a blank."

Visual Love Language Score: Me _____   Partner _____

AUDITORY (HEARING) LOVE LANGUAGE

__ I need to hear the words "I love you" to feel loved.

__ I talk constantly about everything and have an opinion on every subject.

__ I like hearing and saying "I love you" many times a day.

__ I feel it's very important to "talk things out."

__ I feel that if you talk to me, that means you love me.

___ To me there is no such thing as a "rhetorical question"—I answer everything.

___ I love music and poetry.

___ I speak with a certain rhythm or variations in tone.

___ I am very sensitive to others' tone of voice.

___ I hum, whistle, talk to myself a lot.

___ I have the radio or TV on at all times, "just for the noise."

___ Sounds (music, tone of voice) affects my mood.

___ I get turned on by romantic/emotional and/or sexual conversations.

___ When arguing, I often don't know when to stop. I might follow the other person from room to room talking, whether or not the other is listening.

___ When moderately stressed I try to talk about it. When maximally stressed, quiet is the only thing that will restore me.

___ The phone is almost permanently connected to my head.

___ I always try to have the last word.

___ I use comments like "hear me out," "I could tell by your tone," "I need some feedback," "we need to talk," "just listen to me," "it made me want to scream," and other auditory metaphors in speech.

Auditory Love Language Score: Me ___   Partner ___

KINESTHETIC (TOUCH) LOVE LANGUAGE

___ I feel that you love me if you're touching me.

___ I love when we're both quiet and we can just *be* together.

___ I feel that we shouldn't have to talk all the time or work so hard on our relationship."

___ I like touching and hugging more than any other expression of affection.

___ I dress for comfort. Appearance is secondary if considered at all.

___ I am easily overwhelmed in verbal conflict and often feel picked on. I never know what to say.

___ I have a hard time making decisions. I tend not to reason things out but give gut reactions to things.

___ I am a poor organizer.

__ I give minimal responses. I tend to gesture, grunt, and shrug more than talk.

__ I work off stress physically, either by exercising or by taking "spa time" (hot bath, pampering, naps).

__ I get turned on by touching, hugging, kissing, massage, and other physical contact. I may have a hard time not "going all the way" when physical affection starts.

__ After arguments, I look for physical reassurance (hugs or sex) to make sure "we're still okay."

__ I love sports and other physical activities.

__ I hate making plans because I don't know what I'll feel like doing on a particular day.

__ It's sometimes hard to motivate me because I can't get past how I feel right now, in a particular moment.

__ I learn by doing.

__ I don't like to read; I prefer and movies with "action."

__ I say things like "get a grip," "I'll handle it," "take it easy," "we really connected," "I just feel that way, that's why," and other physical metaphors in speech.

Kinesthetic Love Language Score: Me _____   Partner _____

In which category did you check the most statements?
Me _____   Partner _____
These are your primary love languages.

In which category did you check the second-most number of statements?
Me _____   Partner_____
These are your secondary love languages.

Which category had the least number of checks?
Me _____   Partner _____
These are your tertiary love languages.

Crossed Wires

As you can see, the differences between love languages are remarkable. Having a different primary love language than your spouse can lead to a great deal of miscommunication. The main reason for this is that people who are masters of one love language tend to disregard or devalue the others because they literally don't make "sense" to them. For example, if you have a primarily auditory love language, you may say, "I love you" many times per day to your more visual mate, and while this is very meaningful to you, he will probably be thinking, "It's easy for her to *say* how much she loves me, but I wonder why she never does anything to *show* me." Conversely, your more visual mate may write you notes, give you cards, and be very conscious of creating a romantic atmosphere, but as much as you appreciate these things, you may be suspicious of him because "He doesn't ever *tell* me how he feels" (visual people tend to live in their heads).

Alternatively, imagine that you are married to a kinesthetic lover, who has the most underappreciated, least understood love language. (Incidentally, the kinesthetic love language tends to be thought of as the "typical guy" style, but remember, at least 20 percent of women display these characteristics as well.) Kinesthetic spouses tend to be very physical. They literally need to "be in touch" with their partners to "feel connected." They can never get enough touching, holding, hugging, kissing, cuddling, or lovemaking. They do, however, max out fairly quickly on conversation (evidenced by the glazed look they get in the presence of highly auditory people) and don't tend to appreciate many visual romantic gestures (cards, flowers, pretty wrapping paper) because they are simply not functional. People who have a primarily kinesthetic love language tend to love quiet times together, just sitting, being, and holding. That's not to say that kinesthetics are lazy (quite the contrary, they are often very hard workers), they just aren't super-showy about their love. They tend not to say much or be very talented at the things many people would consider to be romance. For the kinesthetic, romance is best demonstrated by faithfully carrying out the common duties of daily life. The best kinesthetic lovers are usually very good at quiet, humble service. (Contrast this with auditory people who tend to ask for feedback about everything they do or visual lovers who want to make sure you saw their gesture.) Most often, to demonstrate their affection for you, kinesthetics will do things to make your life easier. They will get you coffee, wash your car, clean the house, pay the bills. Visual and auditory spouses often hate this; they are usually very critical of their kinesthetic partners for trying to get relationship points for "doing stuff they would just have to do anyway." Visual and auditory people tend to believe love is something you have to make a fuss about. Kinesthetic spouses, on the other hand, tend to view love as something they live, feel, and are. "Why do we have to try so hard all the time/analyze everything. Can't we just *be* together?"

When stressed, the purest kinesthetics tend to withdraw into themselves, work, or exercise. Kinesthetics tend to come across as stoic and aloof until you get to know them. They are the people who like to hang on the edge of a crowd and remain quiet until they feel comfortable with their surroundings. Kinesthetics are often criticized as being unemotional, but nothing could be further from the truth. In fact, because their sense of touch is so acute, they tend to feel emotions in their body more strongly and deeply than either visual people (who tend to live in their heads) or auditory people (whose feelings change with the subject they are discussing). The problem is, the purest kinesthetics don't show their emotions or talk about them. They just feel them. In arguments they may be easily overwhelmed and may either agree with their partner to just to shut them up, or react explosively when they just couldn't keep it in anymore. Kinesthetics tend to be impulsive, making decisions based on how they feel at the moment. They often have an intense dislike for schedules insofar as they hate committing themselves to anything they might not feel like doing later. Again, contrast this with auditory people who love to debate everything and visual people who would post their daily schedule in the shower (in triplicate) if they could—because if they can see it, they know it will be done correctly.

To further illustrate the difficulties which can arise when two primary love languages collide, allow me to give you a personal example. I tend to be highly visual (my primary love language), but I am also auditory (my secondary love language). My wife, on the other hand is highly kinesthetic (primary love language) *and* highly auditory (secondary love language). We really connected when it came to our love of long conversations, saying "I love you" a hundred times a day, and all that auditory stuff, but when it came to other areas, we kept missing the boat. I would bring home cards and flowers and she would say, "Thank you, honey" and leave them sitting on the table for a week. How insensitive, I thought. Such things should be displayed prominently on the mantle so that all the world could see how much I loved her. How dare she just let them sit there!

Meanwhile, my wife would sit on the couch and say to me, "Come hold me. Why do we have to always be running somewhere? Let's just sit together."

Please understand, I am much different than I used to be, but back then my definition of hell was "sitting still." It wasn't that I didn't want to sit with her, it was just that everywhere I looked, I saw something else that had to be done. And once I saw the dust on the table, or the crooked picture frame, I just had to fix it or it would make me crazy until I did. Until my wife and I started learning about love languages, we just felt that the other person was being an intractable idiot.

ME: I wish you would get me some flowers or a card sometime [like I do for you].

WIFE: Anybody can do that. Come here, let me hold you.

ME: Hold me? Gee, a whole lot of thought goes into that!

*   *   *

ME: Let's make plans for Saturday. [Visual people can't stand to look out into the future and see a blank space on their mental calendar.]

WIFE: Can't we just see how we feel when we get up? [Kinesthetic people can't stand to be committed to something they might not feel like doing later.]

ME: I don't understand. Why can't we plan something for a change?

WIFE: Why do you have to be so uptight?

No matter how many times we tried to explain our positions to one another they never made sense. Our brains were literally not wired to fully comprehend the information we were giving each other. It was getting to the point where we each began thinking that the other was thoughtless, inconsiderate, "just didn't love me enough to remember what was important to me," or worse. Once we learned what our love languages were, we began to understand that the reason we weren't being loving in as meaningful a way as possible (we were working hard, not smart) wasn't that we didn't love each other enough. We were simply wired differently, and once we learned how to do it, we could "rewire" ourselves to increase our understanding of the true depth of love that existed between us.

People often express surprise that they can rewire themselves to speak and even appreciate another love language. Considering that love languages are based on the way we are wired neurologically, people tend to assume that since they can't physically take their nerves and connect them to new parts of their brain, they can't change their love language. But the truth is we can change our wiring because, to a greater degree than most people appreciate, we are wired by our experiences. Experiences as simple as talking and thinking have profound effects on the structure and chemistry of our neurology. As an example, one fascinating study described in Dr. Jeffry Schwartz's book, *Brain Lock,* showed that after twelve weeks of cognitive-behavioral therapy (basically, a whole lot of "fake-it-till-you-make-it"), sufferers of obsessive-compulsive disorder (some sample symptoms include obsessive hand-washing, hair-pulling, light-switch checking) not only improved behaviorally, but also showed visible changes in their brain activity on a Position Emission Tomography (PET) scan. The subjects in the study were able to rewire the caudate nuclei of their brains just by acting differently for twelve weeks. Rewiring, whether for increased mental health or for increased proficiency in a love language, is more than possible. It is something we do every time we open ourselves up to a new set of experiences.

Since almost everyone has five senses, almost everyone is capable of rewiring themselves to become more fluent in each of the love languages. In fact, even though you are most proficient in one or two of the love languages, you probably already have at least some fluency in all five. But whether or not you fully develop your capacity for the other love languages (and in turn, manifest the fullness of Exceptional Rapport) depends upon how dedicated you are to giving Exceptional Service in your marriage. You may remember that in the beginning of this chapter I wrote that Exceptional Rapport was one way that the service of the soul (that is, that willingness to push beyond your immediate comfort and skill levels to attend to the mental and spiritual well-being of your mate) manifests itself. Over the next few pages, this concept will become clear to you as you discover the steps to achieving Exceptional Rapport in your marriage.

Who You Are Versus What You Like

Couples in less-than-exceptional marriages tend to confuse who they are with what they like. To varying degrees, husbands and wives in Conventional and Shipwrecked marriages tend to hide out behind phrases like, "I'm just not the kind of person who…," or "That's just not me" when their spouses ask them to share certain interests or express their affection in certain ways.

But liking or not liking sports, shopping, lingerie, classical music, monster truck rallies, emotional conversations, floral shows, ballet, fast food, public displays of affection, or the color orange has nothing to do with who you *are,* it is simply a list of things you like or dislike. If you are attempting to build your marriage around a marital imperative, then who you are is a loving, generous, wise, nurturing person, who may not like sports, shopping, lingerie, classical music, monster truck rallies, emotional conversations, floral shows, ballet, fast food, public displays of affection, the color orange, or any number of things, but is willing to involve yourself in such things, for the sake of your mate, because by doing so you become a more loving, generous, wise, nurturing person.

Conventional and Shipwrecked couples tend to have a difficult time with this because they regularly confuse who they are with what they like or do. They tend to worry about "losing themselves" by participating in activities that are not immediately desirable to them. In some ways, they can be just like the two year old who sees himself as "the boy who eats open-faced peanut butter sandwiches with the crust cut off" and throws a fit when you try to give him a put-together sandwich with crust. But in order to have an Exceptional marriage, we need to evolve beyond this point.

How this applies to love languages is simple. If you prefer to give and receive love through one love language, then the demonstrations of affection through a different love language may seem silly, undesirable, even grotesque to you. If you are a more visual person, it just seems obvious to you that if you really love someone, then the thing to do is to write notes, give little presents wrapped in pretty paper, find cute cards. It would never occur to you to think any differently, because you are neurologically wired to give greater weight to visual expressions of love than any other kind of love. It literally does not make sense to you to think any other way. But if you are married to an auditory person, then she may be mildly appreciative of all your visual expressions, but she knows in her mind that if you really loved her, you would engage in all night conversations about nothing, or say "I love you" every time you turned around, or sing her silly love songs. She is neurologically wired to give greater weight to auditory expressions of love. What happens is that you are both working very hard to demonstrate your love for one another, but much—if not all—of your effort is going unnoticed or unappreciated. Recognizing this, you must now choose from two options.

The first choice, and the seemingly more reasonable choice if you are a person who confuses what you like with who you are, is to say that you and your mate are simply "different people," that "nothing is perfect," including your relationship, and that even though you know what expressions of love are most meaningful to your mate—because you have been told forty bizillion times—you simply can't bring yourself to do them because, after all, "I'm just not the kind of person who does that sort of thing." From this point on, your relationship will either exist in a semi-blah state of we've-gone-as-far-as-we-can-go-together-and-since-this-is-as-good-as-it-gets-we-might-as-well-stick-it-out, or you will get fed up and divorce.

The second choice, the choice of the Exceptional spouse, is to say that it is less important that I convince myself that I love my mate (by only doing things that make sense to me), and more important for my mate to know that I love him. Therefore, the Exceptional spouse may continue to do those things she always did to show, tell, or demonstrate her love for her mate, but she will also learn to do the things that are meaningful to him—even if they are completely unmeaningful to her. The person taking this approach does not "lose herself" any more than an Englishman loses himself by saying *"Je t'aime"* to his French lover instead of "I love you." After all, he is saying the same thing, only in a different language. When we demonstrate love to our mate in a way that is meaningful to them, instead of limiting ourselves to those ways which are meaningful to us, our loving efforts make a greater impact on our spouse—because we are now speaking their language—and we become, literally, more sensual people ourselves, open to the sights, sounds, textures, tastes, and scents of the world like we never could be when we limited ourselves to our own preferred sensory language.

Becoming Multilingual

The following are some suggestions for activities that demonstrate love in either a visual, auditory, or kinesthetic way. Review and discuss them with your mate. Which would he or she like you to do more of?

Which would you like your mate to do more of for you? What are some of your own ideas for novel visual, auditory, or kinesthetic expressions of love?

Increasing Your Visual Love Language

If your mate has a primarily visual love language and you want to show your love, try the following:

Write love notes.

Buy or make an "I love you" card. Just because.

Have a glamorous, professional photo taken and give it to your mate.

Learn to tie bows and wrap gifts decoratively.

Keep all clutter out of sight. Concentrate on making your home "look tidy" even if it really isn't.

Leave love messages on Post-it notes and stick them all over your home and your mate's car.

Read books together.

Have a candlelight meal. Use the good china and silver—even if you're having hot dogs.

Get a blanket. Lie out under the stars at night and count constellations, or make up your own.

Wear lingerie or attractive pajamas to bed.

Make love with the lights on.

When making love, spend lots of time on foreplay.

Keep the bedroom free of laundry and clutter.

Look into each other's eyes and don't say anything for a whole minute.

Have lots of candles in your bedroom, bathroom, or on your mantel.

Go to a movie together.

Make a silly video of you and your beloved making snow angels, building sand castles, baking a cake, or whatever. Make popcorn and watch the video later.

Make a sign that says "I Love You!" and hang it from the door.

Dress up in your best clothes for a date with your mate. Even if you are just going to the mall. Don't worry about overdressing; look good for your mate.

Buy flowers regularly. They don't have to be expensive; anything pretty and thoughtful will do.

Write your own card at one of those "Create-a-card" places.

When you look at your mate, smile.

Increasing Your Auditory Lovestyle

If your mate has a primarily auditory love language and you want to express your love more effectively, try the following:

Say, "I love you" several times a day. Say it in a genuinely loving tone.

Call your partner from work as often as you can just to say, "Hi."

Regularly compliment the things your mate does and the way he or she looks.

Read aloud to one another.

When making love, talk about how your mate is making you feel. Say what you like; make noise.

Make an audiotaped "love note." Put it in your mate's car stereo so that it automatically clicks on when he or she is driving to work.

Leave cute messages on the answering machine.

Buy your mate CDs of music you think he or she would like.

Compliment your mate publicly. Don't ever criticize your mate in public.

Tell your mate how glad you are that you are married. Be prepared to answer why you think this way.

Ask your mate's opinions. Listen respectfully. Contribute to the conversation.

Make a habit of remembering jokes and stories from your day. Share them with your mate.

Talk about current events.

Whisper "sweet nothings" in your partner's ear.

Give your spouse a "pet name." Use a silly voice when you say it.

Be very careful of your tone of voice.

On stressful days, be available to talk but keep noise to a minimum.

Buy your mate an "ocean waves" tape to listen to at bath time.

Write a song and sing it to your mate. Write a love letter or poem and read it aloud.

Hum your mate's favorite love songs.

Auditory people remember every single word that comes out of your mouth, so learn to choose yours carefully.

Increasing Your Kinesthetic Love Language

If your partner has a primarily kinesthetic love language and you want to demonstrate your love more effectively, try the following:

Hold your mate's hand often.

Sit on the same piece of furniture with your mate (instead of across the room).

Kiss and hug your mate several times a day.

Spend a quiet evening just sitting together watching the tube. Don't talk. Give your mate the clicker! Don't complain about his or her choices.

Snuggle.

Give your mate massages.

Scratch your mate's back. Rub your mate's neck.

When at home, or if you're sure no one is looking, pinch your mate's butt.

Nibble your mate's ears.

Work side by side on a household project or other fun activities.

Don't talk while making love. Don't tell your mate what you want. Instead, take your mate's hands and passionately demonstrate what you like.

Be sexually assertive.

Skip foreplay once in a while and "go right to the good stuff."

Wear nothing to bed. Turn off the lights. Make your mate feel his or her way around.

Cuddle under the blankets together.

Give your mate a "spa day" to be alone, soak in the tub, exercise, do a face mask, whatever your mate needs to recharge his or her body.

If your mate likes to watch or play sports, learn to love watching or playing too.

Go to a bath and body store. Stock up on massage lotion, bubble bath, and other comfy stuff.

Don't pick on your mate when he or she wears that ratty and old but very comfortable whatever it is.

Some General Tips

1. If your partner has indicated a preference for something on the above lists, do it. Write the items you checked above on your Twenty-five Ways to Make Love—Every Day list (page 90). It

doesn't matter if a particular affectionate gesture makes sense to you. It doesn't matter whether you happen to like those things or not. It doesn't even matter if you think your mate deserves it or not. You claim to love this person. Love means working for your mate's good. Now that you know what he or she thinks is good, get to work.

2. Don't ever criticize your mate for behaviors and preferences related to a love language. If you do, you might as well smack your mate in the head with a board while you are at it. Since a love language is so personal, criticizing it will be taken very personally. Don't criticize.

3. Challenge your comfort level. If a particular request is not offensive to your dignity or your value system, then fulfill that request. We have to love our mate even when it makes us uncomfortable. "That's just not me..." or "I'm not comfortable..." aren't good enough. Stop whining. You'll never get comfortable sitting on the edge of the pool; you've got to stick your toe in—at least.

4. There comes a time in every couple's life when they are getting as much intimacy as they are going to get from their lives unless they really shake things up. Becoming fluent in a second and third love language is a great way to do this. It stretches you to go beyond a merely "comfortable intimacy," and empowers you to develop an intimacy based on actualization.

Let's Get Wired

Rewiring is especially important for avoiding another common problem I encounter with my clients. Specifically, I am referring to the times when husbands and wives have the vague sense that, "something is wrong in my marriage but I don't know what. I know my mate loves me, I just feel like something is missing."

Very often, what's missing is a particular love language, and my client is suffering from a kind of marital sensory deprivation. For example, if you are a primarily kinesthetic lover, your nervous system will literally crave touch. If you are primarily a visual lover, your nervous system craves visible demonstrations of love. If you are primarily an auditory lover, your nervous system aches to hear "I love you" and similar messages. If you don't receive enough loving input through your most acute senses, you will physically feel dried up and dull. Why wouldn't you? The neural pathways which carry loving signals to your brain are dried up and dulled. They are literally atrophying from a lack of stimulation. If this continues over a long period of time, you may become depressed, possibly seriously so. For many, love languages aren't just a cute thing they read about in some book. Love languages can actually mean the difference between mental health and mental anguish. As a husband or wife, you have an immense amount of power to affect the health of your mate's body, mind, and spirit. Will you love your mate the way your mate needs to be loved? The way your identity and marital imperative command you to love? Your marriage: your choice.

You were originally "wired" by your experiences. You "rewire" yourself by participating in experiences that, to this point, you had decided were "just not you." The mechanics of rewiring are simple, but it takes consistent thought and effort. As you learn to appreciate your mate's primary love language, you are literally wearing a new groove in your brain through which, to use a computer metaphor, each of your senses (and in turn your love languages) can interface more effectively with the others. Sometimes, especially when you first begin to work on creating that new groove, you will have to practice some real self-discipline. As you read earlier, the last thing I, as a visual/auditory, busy, productive, noisy, hyperactive person wanted to do was sit still and hold my wife for more than 2.5 seconds. But because I understood this would demonstrate my love to her in a more meaningful way than all the notes I could write and flowers I could bring home, I *made myself* do it.

No doubt there are those of you who think that love should just "come naturally." Well, it does to a degree, but sometimes even the most natural of loves requires a bit of heroic effort to help it along. It was important to me that my wife know how much I loved her, so I sat there and controlled my urge to get up and adjust the crooked picture frame. I resisted the impulse to start gabbing about nothing or making plans for what we were going to do after we were done sitting there. I sat, I held, and you know something? I learned to really like it! Pretty soon I wanted to do more of this "sitting and being quiet thing." Next, I started noticing some kinesthetic tendencies creeping into other areas of my life. I became less compulsive, more able to tolerate petty concerns and offenses. I could relax more easily. I used to be the kind of guy who wore a jacket and tie to bed, and now I found myself (*quelle horreur!*) wearing sweaters and open-collared shirts—to work! I know all this probably sounds pretty silly to you, but I am trying to make a point. In order to grow both as a person and in intimacy with my wife, I had to stop saying, "I am not the kind of person who…" I had to humble myself, tell myself that maybe my wife really did have something to offer that I didn't understand, and then I had to try it. Not just once, but over and over until I developed an appreciation for it as well. Maybe not as great an appreciation as my wife had, but an appreciation nonetheless. I had to try these new experiences until they literally wore a new groove in my brain through which my kinesthetic senses could interface with the vast audiovisual network that I had installed years before.

My old rule was, "I don't do anything that makes me uncomfortable." Now my rule is, "As long as it doesn't violate the qualities I stand for or my moral principles, I'm game." I find that this newer rule encourages me to be a more well-rounded person, a more exciting, vital person, and a better lover to my wife (in and out of bed).

One other very reasonable question springs to mind. You may be wondering, "How did Exceptional couples come to learn all this?" In considering the Exceptional couples with whom I am familiar, two patterns emerge: Either the couple already shared an uncanny fit between at least their primary and secondary love languages, or, more likely, the couple's sense of Exceptional Service propelled them forward in this area without having had to conceptualize what they were doing as learning another love language. As I have mentioned throughout the chapter, Exceptional Rapport is really just another way Exceptional Service manifests itself. If we all truly practiced Exceptional Service in our marriages, then eventually we would come to understand our mates on an exceptional level. Unfortunately, most of us do not. I have found that most of us, myself included, for whom Exceptional Service does not come easily, need a map, a specific plan that shows us where we are, where we want to go, and what we have to do to get there. This chapter—indeed, this entire book—is an attempt to define for the rest of us what, in some cases, seems a very obvious course of action for those "naturally occurring" Exceptional couples. By imitating the masters and "faking it 'til you make it," you and your mate will one day be able to stand face to face, look into each other's souls, and understand exactly what the other is about.

8

Exceptional Negotiation

*In good conversation parties don't speak to the words,
but to the meanings of each other.*

—RALPH WALDO EMERSON

USUALLY, after an argument, Mirra and Sam would be so upset with each other that they couldn't even speak—sometimes for days. Their most incendiary fights occurred when the couple paid their bills each month. But as they sat in my office, they told me that they had some good news for a change.

MIRRA: This month we actually got through it. We got all the bills paid and didn't even scream once.

SAM: Well, it got tense once or twice. But the thing that cinched it was when I wanted to lay into her, I finally did what you said. I took a deep breath, looked at her—and asked if she wanted a cup of coffee or something. It was so out of character for me that Mirra just burst out laughing. She actually thanked me for trying so hard, and the rest of the night—perfect.

MIRRA: It felt good to be on the same side for a change. If it could go like this every month, I might not mind paying the bills with him.

Exceptional Negotiation is the skill that allows Exceptional couples to have arguments that might be best compared to a deep-muscle massage. As one exceptional husband told me, "It hurts a little while you're going through it, but you always feel better in the end, and the relationship seems looser and more comfortable than when you started." Compare this to those couples whose arguments tend to look like boxing matches, or still other couples for whom "compromise" means determining whose turn it is to lose." Through Exceptional Negotiation couples become more intimate partners *because* of their arguments rather than in spite of them.

The Rules

Usually when I talk about Exceptional Negotiation, people get the mistaken impression that Exceptional couple's arguments are pinky-finger-extended tea parties with "please" and "thank-you" all around. This is not quite the case. After all, these are passionate people. Why should their disagreements show any less passion than any other area of their lives? But even the most passionate arguments can be healthy—and exceptional—as long as they follow three basic rules.

Rule 1. The argument must move things along to a mutually satisfying solution. This rule is self-explanatory. Obviously an arguing style is unhealthy if it never resolves anything. Either the couple lacks problem-solving skills or they enjoy beating each other up.

Rule 2. There are certain lines the couple simply doesn't cross no matter how heated their discussions get. Each couple must develop their own, unique "rules of engagement," that is, they must determine those behaviors, tones of voice, words, subjects, which are unacceptable in an argument. For example, some couples refuse to shout. For others, shouting is perfectly acceptable. Some couples draw the line at name-calling, while other couples find that certain names are acceptable while others are definitely off-limits. Each couple must decide for themselves what they will and will not tolerate.

As subjective as this process is, one good rule of thumb is to disallow anything that makes one's mate defensive or quickly escalates the argument. At the very least, such behaviors should be kept to a minimum. When explaining this to clients, one objection I hear is, "Well, I'm okay with (such and such) but she's not!" This is irrelevant. For an argument to be effective and healthy, both spouses must be comfortable with the "rules of engagement." Otherwise, one spouse will feel that he or she is at a disadvantage, which could eventually lead to that spouse "playing dirty" to make up for the imbalance in power, quickly escalating the argument. At the end of this chapter, you will have an opportunity to clarify your own rules of engagement.

Rule 3. In the couple's overall relationship, there is a five-to-one ratio of positivity to negativity, that is, the couple is five times more loving and affectionate than they are argumentative, critical, or complaining. This rule applies to your life together in general, but it is especially important for its impact on your ability to have healthy arguments. The idea that there must be five times more positive interactions than negative ones in your relationship is meant to be taken literally. For every criticism you levy against your mate, you must be five times more complimentary to maintain credibility. For every argument you have, you must have five time more pleasant times together to maintain rapport.

Dr. John Gottman determined the five-to-one rule—the so-called magic number—to be *the* factor which predicted with 95 percent accuracy whether or not a couple would still be together in five years. Following the five-to-one rule in all aspects of your relationship (not just when you are arguing) is essential to healthy problem-solving because it makes certain that your disagreements are conducted in a loving context. In other words, maintaining the five-to-one positivity-negativity ratio maintains your credibility with your mate. It is not an uncommon experience to be called up short by one's mate and wanting to respond with some version of "And who the hell do you think you are?" And yet, if you know that eight times out of ten your mate is a pleasant person who conducts his or her affairs with your best interests in mind, then you will be more willing to listen—without becoming defensive—the two times out of ten your mate is critical of you.

But once you start letting the positivity to negativity ratio become three to two or worse still, one to five, defensiveness, misunderstanding, and resentment increase almost exponentially. The most important part of healthy arguing—establishing a loving context in which to hold arguments—begins long before the actual conflict begins. Credibility is the factor which determines whether your views will be respected or fall on deaf ears. By guarding the five-to-one ratio in your marriage, you enhance your credibility with your mate by looking like a person worth listening to.

Beyond these basic rules, Exceptional couples conduct their affairs—especially their negotiations—with a great degree of mutual respect. They work very hard to maintain their own self-respect as well as a respectful attitude toward their mate. The remainder of this chapter will examine those attitudes and actions which communicate this remarkable respect and can maximize any couple's capacity for Exceptional Negotiation.

Maintaining Your Own Dignity

For Exceptional Negotiation to occur, it is essential to maintain your own composure during a discussion. Simply put, no matter how crazy you think your spouse is acting, you must be able to be proud of your own conduct at the end of the day. Nothing less than your self-esteem is riding on your ability to act in accordance with the values, ideals, and goals that are important to you, even under pressure.

Generally speaking, there are four steps to maintaining your composure when problem-solving with your mate.

Know When to Hold 'Em and When to Fold 'Em

The first thing to do before any argument is to decide whether or not it is really an argument worth having. Ask yourself the following questions to decide whether to hold an argument, or fold it before it starts.

a. Is the thing you are upset about a problem that is going to stop you from fulfilling your values, ideals, or goals? Or is this just a petty offense to your comfort level? If this issue really is a challenge to your values, ideals, or goals, skip to c. If you're "just being petty," go to b.

b. Even though this seems like a petty issue, ask yourself if you are using this petty thing as a way to demonstrate your anger over another, more vital issue. What might that issue be? If you can identify what you're really angry about, go to c. If, on the other hand, you really are just being petty, it's time to take a breath, swallow your pride, and spare yourself and your mate the unnecessary stress. This would be a good time to practice some patience and build credibility with your mate.

c. Well, it looks like some problem-solving is called for. Make some time to sit down with your mate (don't make it an ambush) after you've read the rest of this chapter, you'll know exactly how to get your needs met every time. And, you'll be able to do it gracefully.

Begin With the End in Mind

Would you ever start a business meeting without an agenda and expect to get anywhere? Of course not. In the same way, no couple begins an effective argument without a plan. Too many husbands and wives treat their marital problem-solving sessions like pointless, meandering, bitch sessions. They have nothing more on their problem-solving agenda than "demonstrating my pain and proving what a pig you are." This is a recipe for disaster. Even if you were "successful" in proving your pain and demonstrating your mate's "pigness," then what? Can you really say that such a discussion would do anything except allow you to let off some steam? Would having such a "discussion" actually prevent the problem from ever happening again? Of course not. All you've done is emotionally regurgitate all over each other.

To have an effective argument, you must know the goal you want to achieve by initiating the discussion. Before you open your mouth and say something stupid, calm down enough to at least have some possible answers to the following questions.

1. What do I need to know from my mate to feel better about this problem?
2. What do I think needs to happen so that we can avoid this problem in the future?
3. What changes will I have to make to solve this problem? (That is, what are you willing to do other than tell your mate what to do?)

Only when you have at least some general answers to these questions are you ready to begin an effective problem-solving session. This requires more preparation than most husbands and wives are used to doing before starting an argument, but the payoff is big. By doing this, you protect your self-respect, build credibility with your mate, and increase the chances of getting the solution you want. Compare this to the more typical couple-arguing pattern of (a) scream like idiots, (b) stuff your feelings because you aren't getting anywhere, (c) repeat at later date, and you'll begin to see the wisdom of this approach.

Maintain Your Emotional Temperature

In any problem-solving discussion, you must keep a close watch on your emotional temperature scale. On a scale of one to ten, with a one representing you on some very potent tranquilizers, a four representing how you feel as you are reading this, and a ten representing you at the top of a clock tower with an AK-47, no healthy argument can go on above a 6.5.

Above this point, you begin thinking of your mate first as an idiot, then as the enemy. Also, your heart rate rapidly accelerates to between 100-125 beats per minute and your fight-or-flight response is activated. Once this happens, your discussion becomes increasingly more irrational until things either become vicious, or one or the other of you begins to stonewall (when a person's eyes glaze over and everything that is said goes in one ear and out the other). Either way, nothing useful is going to come out of that discussion until your or your mate's fever is reduced. Unfortunately, once you have crossed the 6.5 threshold, there is no way to shorten the cool-down process. You just have to ride the roller coaster until one of you jumps off—or is pushed. This is why those couples who practice Exceptional Negotiation focus on *preventing* "fevers" rather than trying to clean up after them.

There are two basic strategies which can help you maintain your emotional temperature: time-outs, and red-hot loving.

Time-Outs

The first fever-prevention technique is taking a "time-out," which is different than storming out of the room when you can't stand the stress anymore. A healthy time-out is a break that you take when you are beginning to feel stuck or defensive, but are still in fairly good control of yourself (your temperature is at a six or slightly more). This break does not have to be long, it could be as short as the time you need to take a deep breath, get a drink of water, pray, go to the bathroom, or all of the above. In any case, the break needs to be long enough to help you get control of yourself and think about your next step. If you need to take a time-out for longer than a few minutes, try the following: Say "Honey, I love you and this is important to me, but I need some time to think about this/get control of myself." Then, suggest a specific time to resume your discussion (an hour or two is best but as long as it is a specific time, you can postpone a discussion for up to a day or two) and no matter what, stick to that time. Suggesting a specific time helps your mate know that you are not just trying to put him or her off. This will increase the likelihood that your mate will grant your request for an extension instead of following you around from room to room in an effort to get some kind of reaction out of you. Once again, the key to initiating a successful time-out is that neither your temperature nor your mate's is higher than a 6.5.

Red-Hot Loving

Red-Hot Loving is the practice of doing loving things for your mate even when conflict is threatening to heat things up. It often surprises people when I suggest that they do something loving for their mate when they are arguing. It seems counterintuitive, especially if you think of love as primarily a feeling rather than the act of working for your mate's good. But one of the basic tenets of Exceptional Negotiation is: your mate is *not* the problem. You and your mate are *working* to solve the problem. (In fact, one of the most effective ways to tell when an argument's temperature is going over a six is that you start thinking your mate is the problem.) If my mate is not the problem but rather my partner in solving the problem, why should I not want to be supportive to my teammate, to do something loving to show my appreciation for our working together, to encourage him or her through the conflict and toward a solution?

Perhaps an analogy would help. Imagine that you are in a meeting with your coworkers and your boss. Things are beginning to get tense. Now, at what point in the meeting do you tell your boss that she is just like her "crazy bitch of a mother"? At what point would it be helpful or appropriate to assault her character, storm out of the room in a huffy pout, burst into tears, or threaten her? Probably at no point. It wouldn't serve anybody well for you to do those things, so you don't do them. (Or, if you do, you are way beyond this book's scope.) Instead, you focus on the problem and work together toward a solution. When things get tense, or reach an impasse, you adjourn for a while, promising to "come back to it later." Maybe you offer to get some of your coworkers some coffee. Or maybe you all go out for drinks. At the very least, you try to reassure each other that you will find a way through, because the bottom line requires you to find a way through. In each of these cases, you may have felt like punching out the guy sitting next to you, but instead you did something to affirm the group. All for the greater glory of capitalism.

But what about working for the greater glory of your marriage? Offering to get your mate a cup of coffee or piece of pie, to give him or her a back rub, to take a walk together while you discuss the problem are all ways to keep your focus on solving the problem and keep your emotional temperature down. Even more simply, you could thank your mate for hanging in there with you, tell him that you love him, say that you are glad the two of you can work together even when things get hard, remind her why she is special to you, ask him if you could give him a hug or hold his hand. These options do not immediately occur to most of us when we are in conflict, but if you are serious about being able to call yourself a loving person, you are going to have to learn to do them. While it is tempting to give love only when we are feeling positively, it is during a conflict that love is needed most. Being loving builds credibility, it strengthens intimacy, and makes your mate truly grateful to be married to such a mature, caring partner.

There are those people who say that they could never do loving things for their mates in an argument because, "I go from zero to ten in an instant" or, "I always start out at a ten in an argument. What can I do?" If you identify with these statements, you need to seek professional help to deal with this serious personal flaw. Chances are you exhibit a lack of self-control, have a high level of perfectionism, perceive yourself as a victim who must lash out toward others before they get you, and tend to disregard another's feelings for the sake of "being right." Your problem is a serious one. For the sake of your own self-respect, the future of your marriage, and the emotional safety of those around you, seek a referral to a good therapist who deals with anger-control problems.

Don't Both Go Crazy at the Same Time

Perhaps the best advice I ever received before I got married was from an elderly husband who told me the secret of his good marriage: "You and your wife should never go crazy at the same time."

If you've been working up a good lather all day, but your insensitive spouse (who has been lathering up all day as well) beats you to the screaming lunatic role, do whatever it takes to bite your tongue and wait your turn. In the meantime, use all the techniques you'll learn in this chapter to gently and lovingly help yourself through the tantrum.

On the surface this might not seem fair, but there are some built-in benefits for you. Helping your mate get though a (nonviolent) tantrum increases your credibility and the likelihood that your mate will hear you out respectfully—and meet your needs more willingly—when you finally do get your turn to speak. Maintaining your cool under fire earns you respect (and makes your mate feel a little guilty to boot). All this translates into greater pride in yourself and eventually, a more sympathetic audience from your mate.

Cooler heads will always prevail. Take turns going crazy.

Respect for Your Mate

Now that we've examined some of the ways Exceptional spouses maintain their own dignity in conflict, let's take a look at some of the ways you can protect your mate's dignity as well.

Assume a Positive Intention

"I have a pretty hot temper," Helen told me. "I always get over it quickly but before I do, sometimes I say some things I shouldn't. Chad's great though. When I lose it, he just looks at me, tells me that he loves me, and asks me not to lose patience with him."

"Helen is a very loving person," Chad explained. "I know her well enough to realize that if she's talking to me like that, she's just frustrated and doesn't know how to get her point across. There's no sense in getting pissed off about it."

Sometimes it is very hard not to think that our partners are out to get us. It is difficult to believe they don't wake up every morning with their Twenty-five Ways to Make My Mate's Life a Living Hell list in hand. But they don't. Your mate loves you, and because of this, under most circumstances, he or she would not hurt you intentionally. Occasionally, one mate will offend another "on purpose," but most often, this is only because more respectful, or perhaps more subtle, attempts at communication have already failed. Think about it, aren't those the only two reasons you ever cause another person pain? Why would it be any different for your mate?

We must train ourselves out of thinking and responding as if our spouse was out to get us. Whenever we experience those negative thoughts like "She is such a bitch," or, "I can't believe that SOB would do that to me," or "He must not really love me," or anything even remotely similar, we must check ourselves because reality tells us that we are thinking irrationally.

When your spouse offends you, in word or in deed, you must do three things: clarify, clarify, clarify. Give your mate the benefit of the doubt. (No, he or she doesn't deserve it, but do it anyway.) Assume you somehow misinterpreted. Say, "I'm sorry. I didn't understand what you meant by that," or, "I really want to give you the benefit of the doubt. Could you please explain why you did/said that?"

For example:

YOUR MATE: Sometimes, you're such a jerk. You make me so angry.
YOU: (Take a breath) I don't understand what I could have done to make you feel that way. Could you please explain?

Notice, nowhere in this example did you admit to or apologize for anything. How could you? You don't even know what your mate is upset about yet. Instead of reacting, you simply assumed that your usually loving spouse would not say such an obnoxious thing unless there was a fairly good reason for it. Because you love your mate and respect his or her opinion, you are going to find out what was meant by the comment instead of immediately jumping down your mate's throat for being so blunt. You are going to make an effort to assume that your mate is not out to get you, but rather has some good information for you, which, unfortunately, he or she has expressed rather indelicately.

Responding to slights and offenses in this manner is rational, firm, loving, and efficient. It lets your mate know that even if he or she *did* mean what was said, you are going to be kind enough to not let your mate act like an ass at your expense. The same principle applies to obnoxious behaviors. The fact is, underlying even the most idiotic and self-destructive behaviors is a positive intention or a need. Even people who attempt suicide don't think about it so much as a self-destructive act as they do a means of relieving stress. When your mate does something you consider obnoxious, inconsiderate, or rude, you must operate under the assumption that they do not actually intend to come across that way. (Come on now, I know you never mean to be obnoxious, inconsiderate, or rude. Let's give up that double-standard, shall we?) Please don't think I am attempting to excuse obnoxious behavior. Finding the positive intention behind an offensive behavior is not an excuse for the behavior; it is a respectful way to begin changing the behavior. For example, if you learn that the intention behind your spouse's temper is that it is the only way she knows to get you to take her seriously, you and your mate can brainstorm some more respectful and efficient alternatives ("I think I'd be more willing to listen to you if..."). If you discover that the reason your spouse isn't pulling his or her weight around the house is because he or she is sitting up nights worrying about something, you can work together to find solutions. Discovering the intention behind a problem behavior is the first step to changing it.

There are ways that you can help your partner move beyond an obnoxious relationship habit and toward a more respectful solution. When your mate consistently did something that you considered obnoxious, thoughtless, or unloving, you used to respond by saying: "You are such a thoughtless pig!" This is what you will try to do from now on...

1. *Assess the positive intention.* Ask your mate, "When you do/say (that obnoxious thing), what reaction are you hoping to get from me?"

2. *Listen to your mate's response.* After some initial confusion (he or she wasn't expecting the question), your mate will tell you the intention behind his or her behavior.

3. *Offer an alternative way to meet his or her intention.* Say to your mate, "Well, I could understand why you'd want that, but if that's what you really need, could you please do a, b, or c instead of what you're doing? I would like to give you what you're asking for, but I'll never be able to bring myself to doing that if you keep going about it the way you've been."

For example:

YOU: When you refuse to speak to me after an argument, what reaction are you hoping to get from me?

MATE: I felt like you didn't care about what I had to say, so what's the sense of talking to you?

YOU: (Take a breath. Try to understand.) I'm still not sure I understand. What do you need from me?

MATE: I want you to stop trying to force your ideas down my throat and listen to me.

YOU: I never meant to give you that impression. (Aha! See? Your intention was misunderstood.) It really is important to me that you know I care about what you have to say. Could you do me a favor?

MATE: What.

YOU: Since I don't know when I'm doing that, the next time, could you just tell me, "Your not listening!" It would sure help me change a lot faster than your pouting after an argument.

MATE: (Suspicious, but considering how well you've responded, is willing to give you a chance.) If you really think that'll work, I'm willing to try it.

YOU: Great. I promise. I love you.

MATE: I love you too.

Granted, this kind of maturity in problem-solving is difficult to achieve, but it must be done. You may have to repeat this several dozen times before the lesson sinks in. Be patient and respectful. Look for the positive intention behind your mate's offensive words and actions, and work with your mate to find more respectful alternatives to meet his or her needs. Then you will experience the transforming power of your love for one another.

Avoid Showing Contempt

Nothing escalates an argument faster than a little contemptuous gesture or phrase. Some examples include rolling your eyes at your partner, shaking your head in disbelief, agreeing with your mate so he or she will shut up, storming out in anger, letting arguments become even mildly physical, stonewalling, name calling. One of the worst examples of a contemptuous act is threatening divorce.

Threatening to divorce your mate in the heat of an argument makes you look juvenile, petulant, spoiled, pathetic, whiny, and contemptible. While you're at it, you might as well hold your breath until you turn blue. Not only does threatening divorce destroy your credibility, it undermines your mate's ability to trust you, damages the security of your relationship, and offends the dignity of your marriage. (Can you tell this is a pet-peeve of mine?)

Anytime you are tempted to demonstrate any of the contemptuous behaviors I listed above, especially threatening divorce, remember the acronym, DUMM (Don't Undermine My Marriage!).

Don't Nag—Solve!

Your well-meaning spouse doesn't want to disappoint you, and so he sometimes promises more than he can deliver. This leaves you disappointed and resentful. How to solve this problem? The first tack most of us take is to try to bully our mate into keeping a promise. But nagging, pestering, cajoling, and criticizing to get your mate to do something for you demeans both you and your mate and poisons the marriage. In the future, instead of asking your spouse to do something for you and then becoming angry if your mate forgets or neglects your request, assume a positive intention for the oversight and have an alternative plan in mind. What you used to do...

YOU: Honey, can you do (such and such) for me?
MATE: Uh-huh.

Three weeks later, your request is still unfulfilled and you must either begin nagging, or give up and assume that you will never get your needs met.

What you will do from now on...

1. *Set an arbitrary deadline.*

YOU: Honey, I need to get such and such done. I'd really like your help, but I'd like to have it done by Tuesday. Can I count on you? Or should I call a friend (or a professional) to do it?
MATE: Huh? Oh, yeah. I'll take care of it.

Tuesday comes and your spouse has forgotten. Don't say anything.

2. *Call for help.* First thing Wednesday, call the plumber/housekeeping service/automechanic/landscaper/friends or whomever, and ask for their help. Your spouse will come home to find the task done and will either be relieved or irritated. Either response is okay. If your mate is irritated, simply say in your most sincere, innocent voice, "I'm sorry, honey. When you didn't do it by the day you said you would, I

just assumed you didn't have time. Rather than pester you, I thought I'd do you a favor and take care of it."

Granted, this technique may cause some short-term tension, but it solves the problem. It lets your mate know that (a) you mean what you say; (b) you're not going to wait around forever for help; (c) it really is okay if your spouse can't do something for you. You simply need him to be honest about it and help you figure out an alternative way to address your need.

Compare this option with the long-term tension and resentment that accompanies nagging/whining/pestering, which not only doesn't solve the problem, but also causes the heart of a marriage to rot. The fact is, if you need to have something done, the most you can rationally do is invite your mate to help. If he or she can't do it, simply come up with an alternate plan for getting it done. This idea will be strongly repulsive to anyone who is committed to domestic score-keeping in their marriage (or for that matter marital chicken), but to have a Partnership marriage or better, we need to overcome our desire to be taken care of and learn how to become experts at making plans to take care of our own needs. We've got to stop making every little thing be yet another test of our mate's devotion. Of course your mate's help is a gift that should be given freely and generously. But like any gift, you can desire it, and you can be grateful when it is given to you, but—sadly, perhaps—you have no right to demand it.

Never Question the "What," Only the "How" and "When"

You are a spouse, not a parent. It is not your job to ever give or deny permission for your mate to do or have anything. It is merely your job to raise concerns about your mate's plans, taking care to do so supportively, and respectfully. Use the following rule: If you never question the "what," only the "how" and "when," you will never tell your grown-up spouse that something he or she wants or needs cannot be had. You will simply state the conditions (the "how" and "when") under which you would be comfortable helping your partner get that "what." For example:

YOUR MATE: Honey, I would like to start an ostrich farm.
What you used to say: Are you nuts! Why would you want to do that?

What you will say from now on: Well, I guess I'd be okay with that
as long as we could work out (insert your concerns here). What
are your thoughts about the concerns I raised?

Expressing your concerns or objections in this manner lets your
mate know you care both about him or her and about the big picture.
Feel free to be very firm about requiring your concerns to be
addressed even while supporting your mate in the pursuit of his or
her goals. After all, for your marriage to become more intimate, you
both must learn to respect each other's needs while pursuing your
own dreams, goals, and values. This technique is the essence of a
good partnership. In fact, mastery of this skill is one of the things that
separates Partnership and Peer couples from more Conventional
couples. Don't ever issue an edict that your mate can't have or do
something. Do raise your concerns and let your mate decide whether
or not what he or she wants is worth the work it will take to get it. If
your mate decides it's not worth it, then he or she has freely chosen to
pass on the idea. On the other hand, if your mate decides to figure out
a way to address your concerns, then your mate has you to thank for
helping fulfill his or her dreams, goals, or values in a way that is
respectful of the entire family.

Remember, never negotiate the what. Always be willing to negotiate the how and the when.

All You Need Is Love

At this point, many of you are shaking your head in disbelief and
thinking, "I'm sorry, but normal people just don't act like that." And
you are absolutely right. The Exceptional 7 percent are not normal,
that's what makes them exceptional. But, presumably, if you are
reading this book, there is some small part of you that wants to be odd
too, just the same way those Exceptional couples are. You want a
partner, a friend, a passionate lover, a teammate. You want to love your
mate so much it makes other people physically ill (go on, admit it).
You want to be the kind of couple that loves each other so much that
other husbands and wives smack each other after you leave and say to
their mates, "Why can't *you* be that way with me?"

Well, I have some good news: You can have all that and more. All it
will cost you is your obsessive need to be right, your pettiness, your

self-centeredness, and your arsenal of spiteful put-downs. And, as my way of saying thanks, keep as a free gift the "new improved you" that results. Better still, you don't have to make all these changes all at once. You can do it the easy-pay way. Simply pick one of the tips you just read about and start working on it now. A couple of months down the line, pick a new negotiation skill, and work on it. Eventually, you and your mate will learn to let your marital imperative guide you through your conflicts and toward respectful solutions. You will learn how to let the problems you encounter as a couple massage your marriage into something more flexible, more comfortable, and, ultimately, more intimate.

There is a great deal to know about effective problem solving and this chapter has only begun to scratch the surface. Even so, the thought of trying to remember all the tips presented in this chapter during an argument is a bit daunting to most people. Take heart. One word is all you need to remember to begin practicing Exceptional Negotiation today. The word is LOVE:

L   Look for the positive intention.
O   Omit contemptuous phrases and actions.
V   Verify that what you think was said is what was meant to be said.
E   Encourage each other through the conflict and toward a solution.

Use LOVE as your mantra when you and your mate are engaged in those heated problem-solving sessions. What does it profit you to win the fight, but lose your love? Love is the most important rule and the first concern of couples engaged in Exceptional Negotiation. The following exercise will summarize the secrets to Exceptional Negotiation by helping you meditate on the ways LOVE can make you and your mate better negotiators and better people.

Look for the Positive Intention

Identify two things that irritate you about your mate and write them down. Discuss these issues with your mate. Work together to find the positive intention and alternatives. Use the following format:

a. Say: When you (state their behavior) I feel (state your reaction), but I know that you probably don't mean to (hurt, disappoint, frustrate) me. What are you really trying to do?

b. Your mate should tell you the intention. It should be stated succinctly and positively. For example, "I'm trying to get your attention"; "I'm trying to let you know how overwhelmed I am." *Note:* "I don't know" doesn't count. It usually means "I'm embarrassed to tell you." Reassure your mate that you really want to understand and try again.)

c. Now, the two of you must work together to discover a more effective or respectful way to meet that intention. For example, what's a better way for your mate to get your attention? to enlist your help? to let you know you are hurting your mate's feelings?

d. Address any concerns you have about the practicality of these new alternatives. In other words, what would have to happen to make these alternatives stick?

e. Make a promise to live up to the new changes. Hold yourself accountable for your word.

Omit Contemptuous Phrases and Actions

On the left are some of the ways we show contempt to our mates. Circle the ones that you fall victim to. Then, look on the right to find the respectful alternatives Exceptional Negotiators practice.

Contemptuous Act	*Loving Alternative*
1. Rolling your eyes at your partner	1. Making good eye contact
2. Name calling	2. Saying, "Thanks for sticking with me through this"
3. Storming out in anger	3. Taking a respectful, time-limited break from the discussion
4. Threatening divorce	4. Promising that you will keep working on your problems until they are solved—"We're a team after all"
5. Trying to "one up" your mate to see who's hurt whom more	5. Saying, "I'm sorry" for causing your part of the hurt

6. Belittling your partner's thoughts and feelings

6. Saying, "I'm sorry, I don't understand. But I'm trying. Please tell me again"

7. Pretending to agree just to shut your mate up

7. See 6 *or* taking a respectful break until you've calmed down enough to listen

8. Hounding your mate for an answer he or she isn't ready to give

8. Giving your mate the time needed to think things through

9. Letting an argument become physical

9. Taking time-outs; practicing red-hot loving

10. Telling your mate that he or she can't have or do something that is important to him or her

10. Expressing your concerns that would need to be addressed before you would be comfortable helping your mate get or do that important thing.

List your own personal "gotcha's" (and their more loving alternatives). Remember, when you are tempted to show contempt, think DUMM (Don't Undermine My Marriage!).

Verify That What You Think Was Said Is What Your Mate Meant to Say

This involves a similar process to looking for a positive intention. Remember, it doesn't benefit your mate to hurt you. Practice assuming your partner's innocence.

When you feel slighted or defensive, immediately tell yourself to *"Stop!"* Take a breath. Then ask your mate as respectfully as possible, "What did you mean when you said that?"

Practice: Think of a recent time your mate said something that you took offense to. What was he or she really trying to say? Don't guess. Ask. Then return to "Look for the Positive Intention" to brainstorm new, respectful alternatives.

Encourage Each Other Through the Conflict and Toward a Solution

It doesn't take much for even the most well-intentioned problem-solving sessions to get very hot very fast. Here are some things you should be saying to each other to keep things on track. Remember, your mate is not the problem: The *problem* is the problem. Work with your mate to solve the problem.

The following are some statements you might like to use more often in your marital problem-solving sessions. Perhaps you can think of others that best apply to you.

- I love you.
- We're going to get through this.
- Let's work together.
- Let's take a break.
- Can I hold you for a minute?
- We're starting to pick on each other; let's stay focused on solving the problem.
- It's important to talk about that too, but let's stick to one thing at a time.
- Give me a minute, I'm starting to lose it.
- I'm sorry, what I really meant was…
- This is really hard, but you're worth the effort.
- Please be patient with me.
- What you want is important to me.
- When we finish, let's go to dinner/play a game/take a walk.
- Sometimes marriage is a lot of work, but I wouldn't want to be working with anyone else.
- You are so important to me.
- Did I mention that I love you?
- That reminds me of a funny story.
- We're a really good team.

Discuss the following:

- Are you and your mate maintaining a five-to-one ratio of positivity to negativity in your marriage? What steps would you need to take in order to improve it?
- What rules would you say currently guide your arguments?
- What new rules would you like to establish?
- What specific ways could you use time-outs and red-hot loving to decrease your emotional temperature in conflict and encourage teamwork?

Make the following pledge to each other:

I am sorry for the times that I have undermined both your respect for me and the strength of our marriage by choosing not to be loving to you when we disagree. From this day forward, I promise to seek to understand you, even before seeking to be understood by you. Even in conflict, I will work for your good. I will treat you as a partner, not as my enemy. I ask only for your patience and your love as I do the work I need to do to remain faithful to this promise.

I love you, and I want to be the partner you need me to be.

Perfecting the art of battle will enable you and your mate to experience greater intimacy *because* of your arguments rather than *in spite* of them. When you encounter problems in your life and marriage, do what Exceptional couples do: Take off the gloves, and give each other a hand.

9

Exceptional Gratitude

Nothing is more honorable than a grateful heart.

—SENECA

ONCE UPON A TIME there was a village nestled at the foot of a mountain. The people in the village took the mountain for granted. It had always been there, it would always be there, and that was that.

One day, a young man and his bride decided to take a picnic outside the village. Staring up at the mountain, the young woman wondered aloud what it would be like to climb to the peak. At first her husband thought she was crazy. But the woman kept on about it and, finally, the young man relented.

At times the climb was difficult. On the one hand, the mountain was not very steep or dangerous to climb; on the other hand, the couple still had to pay close attention to what they were doing to prevent themselves from sliding back down the slope. Eventually, they crested the peak.

The first thing they noticed was the sweetness of the air. It was not at all like the air in the village, which was pungent with the smell of chimney smoke, sweat, and other odors accompanying the busy, purposeful life of the townspeople. Here, the air smelled of wild-

159

flowers and tasted so much like springwater they caught themselves taking gulps of it to fill their parched lungs.

Looking around them, the couple saw the world as they had never seen it before. They had always thought of the little village as a pleasant enough place, but somehow it felt old and common. And yet, from here, the thatched roofs of the village resembled a patchwork quilt, and the smoke rising from the chimneys brought to mind the great spools of thread the old women used to sew the tiny squares of cloth together.

"I never knew it could be so beautiful," said the young woman. Her husband agreed.

Later, they climbed back down the mountain. They wanted to tell their friends and neighbors of the wonderful experience they had had. But most people simply frowned, saying that they had too much to do to spend their days with their heads in the clouds. Even the few who seemed to appreciate the story refused the young couple's invitation to accompany them on their next trip up.

"You're going back?" they would ask. "It sounds lovely, but I don't think I'm really up for such a climb." Finally their friends went back to their work and back to their homes.

That night the young couple decided to do something that would change their lives forever. Over the course of the next few months, the couple kept climbing the mountain, and each time they arrived at the top, they built a little bit more of the cabin they would one day live in until, finally, one day it was complete. The very next day, they packed up their things and moved to the cabin.

That couple still comes into town regularly to buy supplies. And every time they come they tell their friends of the sweet air and the stunning view and how they see things in a way they never had before. But each time, the couple returns to the cabin with only each other's company to share, which is fine by them, because each day at sunrise and sunset the heavens and the earth perform a show that is just for their eyes and all day long they drink their fill of the sweet air.

A Mountain of Gratitude

Practicing Exceptional Gratitude in marriage is like climbing the mountain in the story. People know they could do it and sometimes they even think about trying, but for the most part it just seems silly.

Isn't life difficult enough without having to pay attention to one more thing? "How could I possibly spare a minute from my busy, purposeful life to do even the little bit of work it would take to climb this mountain. We have air here. I've seen flowers before. What's the big deal?"

As true as all that is, it misses an important point: Yes, Exceptional Gratitude requires some effort, but doing the work makes a marriage that much sweeter, allows a couple to breathe more freely around each other, alleviates the drudgery of everyday life, and gives the couple a new perspective on their world.

Another expression of service of the soul, Exceptional Gratitude teaches the couple to celebrate the simple, common acts of service each spouse performs for the other. By doing this, the Exceptional couple acknowledges three important truths:

1. That one's mate remains in the marriage, not for any selfish need or gain, but because he or she daily chooses to be there, to love and to serve. As such, one's mate's very presence is a gift, for which gratitude is an appropriate response.

2. That the couple is daily working together to help each other become the people they want to be when they grow up. Therefore, the couple is able to be grateful for both the good times and the difficult times, because both are opportunities to grow in the values, ideals, and goals which are important to the couple.

3. That, because neither mate is technically required to do any one thing for the other (due to the dance of competence and the permeability of spousal roles in Exceptional marriages), each act of service is seen as a freely given gift for which at least simple gratitude is an appropriate response.

"If there's one thing you could say about us it's that we really appreciate each other," Dominic says, laughing. "I make a point of telling Wendy almost every day how much I appreciate how hard she works at her job and around the house. She does the same for me. Other people might think we're ridiculous for saying 'thank you' for things like making a meal or even picking up after each other, but it makes us feel good. And we work harder to please each other— because we know we can."

Like all the exceptional qualities, Exceptional Gratitude is made possible by the Exceptional couple's pursuit of both greater personal competence and the fulfillment of their marital imperative. These factors prevent the spouse's presence and or any loving service from ever being taken for granted. Some comparisons might help.

In Shipwrecked marriages, spousal roles are very rigid and legalistic. Each spouse has a specifically defined job to do, and each is expected to do that job. While Exceptional couples think nothing of expressing gratitude for each other's cooking a meal, working hard at a career, or any other mundane task of daily life, Shipwrecked couples would never think of expressing thanks for any such thing, "What? You want a medal just for doing your job?"

Since Shipwrecked couples base so much of their marriage on the game of "you scratch my back and I'll scratch yours," they tend to think that they have already paid each other for any services rendered. For example, the traditional Shipwrecked husband thinks the following about his wife, "You can't earn a living. So, by doing it for you, I pay you for your housework and child-rearing. Just mark my receipt 'paid in full.'" In turn, the traditional Shipwrecked wife thinks the following about her husband, "You couldn't cook or keep yourself neat if your life depended on it. I pay you for your work by doing these things for you. So mark my slip, 'paid in full.'"

As a result, when one Shipwrecked spouse wants something more from the marriage—more time, more intimacy, more romance, more sex, more gratitude—the other spouse acts as if they just got a notice that their cable bill was going up by $100 per month. "Oh no you don't," they scream. "We had a deal. And now you're changing the rules in the middle of the game? I don't *think* so." This fair-exchange-for-goods-and-services mentality sets a couple up to take each other for granted. The fairly overt message of this marriage is, "I'm paying you to do your job, so shut up and do it." It would seem that just as mutual dependency poisons love over time, it leaves little room for gratitude.

Conventional couples tend not to suffer as much from this quid pro quo mindset. Some elements of it remain, but they are mitigated for the most part by the fact that Conventional couples' roles are semipermeable. In other words, a Conventional spouse would consider doing "my mate's job" if asked, and if it didn't threaten the balance of power too much. But Conventional couples tend to suffer from a different obstacle to Exceptional Gratitude: fear of "spoiling" the mate and wrecking the delicate balance that guards against either spouse taking advantage of the other. The thinking goes like this, "I really do appreciate all he does for me, but if I make too big a deal about it, he'll get a swelled head, sit on his arse, and make me do everything." Conventional couples often say this—or sentiments like it—with a great deal of humor, but their laughter speaks a real concern. Because the Conventional relationship is based on "equality" and "fairness," if one spouse gives the other spouse more gratitude than might be considered "fair," there is a real fear that the other spouse will interpret this as a sign that he or she is doing "too much" and so, do less in an attempt to right the perceived imbalance of power. ("Wow! She's really grateful for my washing the dishes, I guess I've earned enough points for one day. Time for a nap!") Whether this "spoiling" actually ever happens or not is a subject for debate, but the point is that most Conventional couples fear that it will happen, and so they act as if it would, thus decreasing the amount of gratitude they can comfortably express in their marriage.

One time I was telling a couple I had in counseling, Al and Rena, about Exceptional Gratitude and they decided to have some fun with me. For the next five minutes or so, they proceeded to thank each other for every stupid little thing that happened.

RENA: "Thank you for glancing at me sideways, my dear, it made me feel very special!"

AL: "Oh, indeed! Thank you for your gratitude!"

Now, it just so happened that they had come to the session in a fairly bad mood. I decided to let them go on for a bit before I said, "All right, guys. I know, you think this is ridiculous. But let me ask you a question. How do you feel now, compared to when you came in?"

Al answered, "Well, when I came in, I felt angry. Now I just feel stupid." They both chuckled. (They weren't going to give up that easily.)

I said, "But the fact is, even though you have just been playing at being grateful you do feel better about each other. It was out of the ordinary. It interrupted your usually angry way of dealing with each other. It gave you something to laugh about. Frankly, I would be happy if that's all it did, but just think about how you would feel about each other if you expressed more genuine gratitude throughout the course of every day. Don't you think it would at least improve your sense of humor about each other and your circumstances? Isn't it possible that it could lead to some other good changes as well?"

Five Ways to Create a Gratitude Shift

We talked about this for a while, and though they were still suspicious, they agreed to try it for a week. I gave them five tips for creating a "gratitude shift."

Catch Your Mate Being Good

It is all too easy to focus on the things we don't like about our mates, especially when we are irritated with them. But criticizing too much upsets the "magic number," the five-to-one positivity to negativity ratio, and in turn undermines your credibility with your mate. ("There he goes again. He's never happy. I just let it go in one ear and out the other.")

The only effective solution is to balance any necessary criticisms with at least five times as many compliments and expressions of gratitude. These don't have to be elaborate. In fact, it is better if they aren't. A simple, "Hey, thanks for taking care of that," or "I really appreciated such and such," or even "Your hair looks especially nice today," or similar comments let your mate know that you *are* paying attention. And because everybody loves approval, your spouse will tend to replicate the behavior you are rewarding her for with your gratitude. Professionally and personally, I have learned the power of catching someone being good.

When I was still in graduate school, I did an internship in a "family preservation" program that was specifically designed to help parents with children who were in danger of being placed out of the home, either in foster care or a psychiatric hospital. Our mission was to keep these kids at home whenever possible. Besides actually meeting with the families, part of my internship requirement was to learn about the various ways to do family preservation work. One of my professors explained a model that fascinated me. It was built entirely around "catching the family being good."

A client family would give their permission to be videotaped in their home. The therapists set up the cameras and then left. Once a week someone from the office came by to pick up the family's tapes.

Later in the week, a therapist returned with an edited copy of a tape containing all the family interactions that the clinical team liked. The family then sat down with the therapist to watch the video, discussed what they did *well* in the previous week, and examined why those particular interactions worked.

The study showed that in the period of a few weeks, most families had improved so much that there was no need to remove the children. These "severely dysfunctional families" with horribly incorrigible children changed dramatically, simply because they were consistently caught "being good."

Think of the wonderful fruit this intervention could bear in your relationship. In my own marriage, I know how well I respond when my wife acknowledges something I have done for her or compliments my appearance on a particular day. Besides making me feel good, I like pleasing her, and so I try to do those things more often. I don't think I am unique in this way. Everyone loves approval, but husbands and wives tend to be more stingy with it than they should. As a result, spouses end up feeling unappreciated by and isolated from each other.

If you would like to find out what "catching your mate being good" could do for your marriage, simply add the following to your Twenty-five Ways to Make Love—Every Day list: "Every day, comment on at least five things my mate does for which I am grateful." Chances are you'll surprise yourself and find even more than five. Surprise your mate and tell him or her about what you've found.

Keep a Gratitude Journal

I actually learned this from a client. In order to maintain the changes they had made in therapy, a husband and wife I was seeing decided to keep a notebook together. Every night before bed, the couple would sit together and write down all the things their mate did for them (or was to them) for which they were grateful that day. All of the things they listed were simple. Examples included, "You helped me keep my cool with the kids," or "Thanks for noticing the toothpaste on my chin before I went to work," or "You looked really great in that suit."

But simple as these things were, it helped the couple know how much they appreciated each other. It reminded them of all the little ways they took care of each other every day. Likewise, this exercise had the benefit of increasing many of these desired behaviors. And there was one more bonus the couple hadn't planned on when they started their journaling. Because they did this right before bed, it increased the frequency of this couple's lovemaking. As the wife put it, "Even when I'm tired or had a bad day, I end up feeling so good about him when we do our journal, I can't keep my hands off him."

Sounds good to me.

Look for the Strengths Your Spouse's Weaknesses Bring Out in You

Throughout the book, I have mentioned that Exceptional couples understand how their partners' strengths *and* weaknesses help them become better people. While no spouse wants his or her mate to have shortcomings, the fact is, we all do. Even if we are working to overcome them, from time to time our partner is going to stumble into our flaws and vice versa. In such times, it is a very mature spouse who can see the opportunity for growth these situations present for him or herself. Perhaps the circumstances present an opportunity to grow in patience or graciousness. Perhaps this is an opportunity to become less petty, or more loving, or exhibit more strength of character, or any number of possibilities.

The most profound example of this I ever had the privilege of witnessing was while working as a consulting therapist for a hospice. I would visit the homes of the dying and provide supportive counseling to the patients and their families. Obviously, this was a very stressful time, and while all of the families responded heroically to the caregiving requirements, many had to fight back a great deal of anger and resentment as they watched their loved one deteriorate.

But I will never forget one elderly gentleman—and he was a gentleman—who was taking exceptionally good care of his wife. Moreover, he seemed not to lose his patience like so many other caregivers would sometimes understandably do. I myself have a difficult time watching those I love suffer even from a head cold and, to my shame, I often allow such things to make me an insufferable crab—as if I had anything to complain about. But this man was so patient and loving in his ministrations I finally asked him what his secret was.

"We've had a lot of good years together, and part of it is I figure I owe at least this much to her. But the other thing is that I've never been a very patient person. I used to complain a lot. It was mostly my way of blowing off steam. Anyway, seeing all that she's going through, and considering everything I've had to do, what with taking her to doctors and getting up at night to change her diapers and everything else, the little irritations in life don't seem to bother me so much anymore."

He started to tear up. "After all these years, she's still teaching me things."

I would invite you to look at yourself when your spouse's weaknesses and vulnerabilities are exposed, and see what they can teach you about yourself.

Keep a Balanced View

Dr. Aaron Beck, the original force behind the highly effective treatment model known as cognitive psychotherapy, notes in his book *Love Is Never Enough* that many of the qualities spouses once admired in their mate become the things they most hate about them later in the marriage. So, for example, the man who was laid back before marriage comes to be seen by his wife as lazy. The woman who was sensitive and caring before the wedding is later criticized for being overly emotional. Which perception is true? They both are. Our spouses don't usually become worse as the years go by (although it is tempting for some people to think they do); we simply reinterpret the qualities we once admired.

The trick to dealing with this is trying to keep a balanced view, to remember that many personality traits can be both positive and negative depending upon the context. For example, someone who is a real take-charge person at the office might inadvertently come across as a control freak at home. It all depends on the context.

The Exceptional spouse's job is to keep both sides of his or her partner's qualities in mind. This way, even when you feel the need to address a particular, irritating trait, you can remain grateful for your spouse's good points, and approach your mate in a more respectful way. When trying to raise a concern with your husband or wife, there is a world of difference between, "You are such an irresponsible jerk" and "I'm glad that you're laid back, but sometimes I wish you were a little less laid back."

Act Loving

One other effective way to increase gratitude for your mate is to do loving things for her. Obviously, when you do loving things for your partner she will feel appreciated, but, as you saw in chapter 5, when you do loving things for her, you also feel better about her. Loving behavior drives loving emotion.

If you want to feel more grateful for your spouse, pick out a card for him, give him a back rub, tell him you love them, or find some other wonderful way to let him know how grateful you are that he is in your life. Express your gratitude and your gratitude will flourish.

At their session the following week, Al and Rena said that it had been hard at first to remember not to be critical, but once they started doing their gratitude journal together, it became easier to start "catching each other being good." In fact, they reported that this was the first week in a while that neither Al nor Rena felt like they were walking on eggshells around each other. Even though they still had a great deal of work to do, future sessions went more smoothly because there was less tension between them, more humor, and more teamwork. As Rena said, "Knowing I can do something right in his eyes makes me want to try harder."

Bringing Your Gratitude Home

Some people say, "What if I can't find something to be grateful for about my mate?" I always tell them that they probably aren't looking hard enough. Surely there is one sincere compliment you can make about your spouse's appearance, or how hard she works (in or out of the home) to support the family, or the fact that he remembered to pick up his socks, get your favorite ice cream, hum that song you like, or any other million or so things. Gratitude is not something you should reserve for the grand gestures your mate makes. Gratitude must be expressed in your everyday life. If you are grateful for the simple fact that your mate is still breathing and sharing his or her life with you, for God's sake, say so.

One final objection to Exceptional Gratitude is, "I don't think I'd like that because I'm not very good at taking compliments." Well, don't you think it's time you learned? It seems to me that there are at least a million people we meet every day who in one way or another try to tear us down. Don't you think it would be a good idea to learn to appreciate the one or two people who would like to help build us back up again? If you don't know how to take a compliment, give your mate the blessed opportunity to teach you how, by letting him or her shower you with love. Someday you might just be able to see yourself through your mate's eyes, and you will in turn be able to be grateful to them for helping you find greater self-esteem.

To bring home the message of Exceptional Gratitude, discuss the following with your mate:

- Which of the five ways to increase gratitude do you think you need more of in your marriage?
- What would it be like for you and your mate to begin thinking of the simple things you do for each other not as jobs that you must do to hold up your end of the marital deal but as freely offered expressions of love?
- Are you five times more complimentary than criticizing? Regardless of your answer, how can you do better?
- Describe at least three times in your marriage when you were most confident that your mate valued you. What made these times so special?

After your discussion, do the following:

- Write a letter to your mate that describes how he or she has helped you become the person you are today. Assuming you like the person you have become, thank your mate for helping you grow.
- Give your mate a "Gratitude Party." Go out to dinner and give him or her a few small gifts, each of which should represent something about him or her that you appreciate. For example, a small mirror to represent her beauty, a small handmade certificate for his being thoughtful. The gifts don't have to be expensive but each should show thoughtfulness and gratitude.

Can You Say "Gratitude"? Sure You Can...

I was watching *Mr. Rogers' Neighborhood* with my children one day, when the man himself began singing a song called "There Are Many Ways." It's about all the ways people express love for one another through the simplest acts of kindness. Throughout the song, he was teaching his young viewers that every time they picked up their clothes, cleaned their rooms, listened, or even simply enjoyed life, they were saying "I love you" to their mom and dad. Honestly, I don't envy Mr. Rogers the task of teaching children something their parents too often forget. On the other hand, maybe children can understand the lesson better because they are not yet as jaded as we are.

If there is one thing I want you to take from this chapter, it is to recognize each act of service your mate performs—be it for you, with you, or even simply around you—as another way he or she is saying, "I love you." Recognize it and say "thanks" for it. No, your "thanks" doesn't have to be a big production—but a little production wouldn't kill you. In fact, it will make your marriage that much sweeter, allow you to breathe more freely around each other, alleviate the drudgery of everyday survival, and give you a new perspective on your life and marriage.

10

Exceptional Joy

Joy rul'd the day, and Love at night.
—John Dryden

A LARGE PART of the strength an Exceptional couple draws from their marriage comes from their ability to enjoy the simple pleasures of everyday life; a quality I refer to as Exceptional Joy.

When I ask clients what they want from therapy, frequently they tell me, "I just want to be happy." Usually this means, "I want to feel good, but I don't want to have to work for it." Far be it from me to knock happiness, but truth be told, happiness pales in comparison to Exceptional Joy (except, of course, that you have to work for Exceptional Joy). Happiness is a feeling, a sense of pleasure that comes and goes as circumstances change, but Exceptional Joy is a constant state of being. It is the deep sense of rightness that comes from being in a marriage where all the qualities, from a marital imperative to Exceptional Gratitude, are practiced. When all of these are evident in a marriage, a special sense of safety is established that empowers the couple to celebrate Exceptional Joy.

The Joy of Safety

Sandy and Josh have been married sixteen years and are the parents of four children. Says Sandy, "When I met Josh, I had just gotten out of a difficult, long-term relationship. I really wasn't interested in meeting anybody, but a friend of mine introduced us and we seemed to hit it off right away. Besides his sense of humor, the thing I was most attracted to was his ability to make me feel safe with him. He is very encouraging and he's a great listener. And he's not afraid to help me deal with my fears.

"When I first started falling for Josh, I told him about my previous boyfriend and how he sometimes acted like he couldn't care if I was there or not. For two weeks after that, Josh wrote me a note every day telling me that I was on his mind even when we were apart. If we had a date scheduled, he would give the note to me himself, but other days he would just drop them in my mailbox or leave it on my windshield at lunch time.

"He's still like that. Whenever I have a problem he does more than listen. He helps me find my strength. And I don't think there's been a day in sixteen years that I haven't enjoyed his company."

As Sandy's story shows, a sense of safety plays an important role in a couple's ability to enjoy their life together. To develop a clearer picture of how safety relates to Exceptional Joy, I want you to imagine two different scenarios. First, envision yourself in the driver's seat of your car at the top of a steep hill. As you begin descending the grade, you lightly depress the brake pedal—and it goes straight to the floor. Your brakes have failed. Careering down the highway at top speed, you feel completely out of control, and are screaming in a terrific panic.

Now the second scenario. Imagine that you are on a roller coaster. You are coming over the top of the first hill. A brief jolt, and then— *whoosh!* You are going down the other side, faster and faster. Your stomach is doing a loop, you feel completely out of control, and you are squealing with delight.

What makes the difference? A sense of safety. You might scream yourself silly on the roller coaster, but you know that your life is not in danger. Eventually, you will be able to step off the ride, after which, if you are like me, you will fall to the ground and kiss the pavement. Not so in the car scenario, in which the greater likelihood is that the pavement will soon be coming up to kiss you.

There is so much in life that is beyond our control. But whether you are terrified by that knowledge or actually experience Exceptional Joy in the face of it depends upon your ability to feel safe. What allows an Exceptional couple to experience this safety is knowing that regardless of the difficulties they encounter in life, they can be assured of both the present and future stability of their marriage. People often look surprised when I tell them this. They think that couples who are confident in the stability of their marriages are self-deluded. After all, no one can predict the future, right?

Of course no one can predict the future, but you don't need to be a fortune teller to know that your marriage will be both happy and long-lasting. Whether or not you live in love for the remainder of your days is not dependent on some magical event that could make or break your relationship in the future. Rather, it is dependent upon how you and your mate respond to an unending succession of present moments. As far as marital stability is concerned, there is no future, there is only your choice, right now, to be loving or not to be loving. Each choice in the present leads to another choice and another and another. Either you consistently choose to be loving even when you don't necessarily feel like it and your marriage grows, or you consistently choose not to be loving—especially when you don't feel like it—and you slowly poison your marriage to death. As psychologist Dr. Wells Goodrich once said, "There are no successful marriages. There are only those that are succeeding—or failing." The ultimate outcome is entirely up to your behavior *today.*

Because the Exceptional couple has committed to a marital imperative, they know how they want to act in every present moment, and they make a mutual and concerted effort to live up to these standards. This commitment leads to the safety and stability which allows the Exceptional couple—as I wrote in chapter 2—to be at peace in times of uncertainty, accept themselves and others, be both spontaneous and creative, have a good sense of humor, take care of themselves, and have an open, positive attitude about life. In other words, it opens the door to Exceptional Joy.

Some of you may be tempted to ask why I am singing the praises of safety and stability now, when earlier I was fairly critical of the Shipwrecked Safety marriages, which make the pursuit of safety their chief aim in life.

There are two kinds of safety: static and kinetic. In the story that began the chapter on Exceptional Gratitude you read about two-

groups of people—the couple who was willing to climb the mountain and the villagers who were not. The villagers exhibited a good
case of static safety, which in marriage translates into "thank God I
found someone who will never threaten me, never make any
demands of me, never challenge me, and never shake things up." This
is why I wrote (in chapter 2) that approximately ten years into the
Safety Marriage, when the wife's static safety needs are met and she
suddenly wants more from the marriage, the husband acts as if he has
been betrayed. "You promised that things would always be how they
were when we first got married! How dare you try to shake things up
now. I was just starting to get comfortable!" Static safety is mostly
about finding a quiet place to be left alone.

By contrast, kinetic safety acknowledges that life is a wild ride, but
it allows couples to enjoy the trip. In marriage, kinetic safety translates
into the following statement: "Come on! Let's climb that mountain.
Sure it will be nerve-racking at times, and, yes, one of us might slip.
But it wouldn't be any fun if there wasn't at least some risk. We'll just
tie our lines to each other and keep climbing no matter what. Trust
me. Together we're going to make it."

M. Scott Peck shocked the world when he opened his bestselling
book *The Road Less Traveled* with the words, "Life is hard." The fact is,
hardship and vulnerability are an integral part of life, but a solid sense
of kinetic safety encourages a couple to experience that hardship and
vulnerability as an adventure—an opportunity to grow as people and
grow closer as a couple.

I love whitewater rafting, but I'm no expert by any means. So, I
always make sure to wear the proper safety equipment and go with
people who know what they are doing. I can enjoy the challenges
presented by shooting the rapids because I trust the people I am with
to look out for me. Even if I fall into the drink—and it's happened—I
am not afraid because I trust what they told me to do and I trust the
guides to keep an eye on me. I know that together we are going to
make it. This trust that allows me to take on challenges beyond my
immediate ability exemplifies kinetic safety. In the same way, kinetic
safety allows the Exceptional couple to push themselves beyond their
limits and experience the rush that accompanies the death of self-
limiting fears, the advent of self-discovery, and birth of uncommon
intimacy. It allows them to experience Exceptional Joy.

The Three Gifts of Exceptional Joy

There are three gifts that Exceptional Joy gives to marriage: the desire to share in each other's interests, the ability to celebrate the little things, and a healthy sense of humor.

Sharing Interests

Exceptional husbands and wives enjoy each other's company much more than do other couples. (We touched on this issue in chapter 6, but now let's take a closer look.) This mostly comes from the couple's willingness to go beyond their limits and be open to the new experiences a mate brings to them. From the outside looking in, it often seems that Exceptional couples just lucked out. "They have so much in common! Its amazing." Of course, most Exceptional couples did not just pop out of the womb liking all the same things. Over the years, they were willing to develop competencies in those areas which were important to their mate because they understood that this is exactly the kind of work true love requires of a person. In chapter 6 I told you about Clarissa, who by working to overcome her loathing of sports was able to share in something that was very important to her husband, and her husband, Joe, who was likewise inspired to become more competent in the things that interested her. In chapter 7, I explained how becoming fluent in a love language that is unfamiliar to you increases your ability to enjoy and share all the experiences of life with your mate. By practicing all of these skills, Exceptional couples learn to enjoy many of the activities and interests which are important to their partners.

Permit me to give you two personal examples. My wife is a lactation consultant (she helps new mothers learn to nurse their infants in healthy ways). Now, this might come as a huge shock to some of you (are you sitting down?), but try as I might, I am never going to learn to lactate. This being the case, there are those who might say that if there ever was an interest a wife could have that her husband could legitimately beg off on, this would be it. But I don't happen to see it that way. In the first place, this is something that is very important to her, and because I love her, I can't help myself from wanting to know everything about her—especially the stuff that doesn't come easily to me. As far as I am concerned, if the woman I love loves something, there must be value in it, and I want to know at least something about

it too. To this end, I have attended seminars with her (where I am the
only male within miles), I make a point of reading some of the journal
articles she reads, and I try to ask intelligent questions so I can learn
more about this part of my love's life. Likewise, at the time she was
first learning to be a lactation consultant, she was nursing our
children. I felt that if I was going to be as loving to her as I could, it
was my responsibility to learn as much as I could about nursing so
that I would know how best to support her. I felt that "my part" of the
nursing relationship was to try to nourish my wife emotionally and
mentally as much as she was nourishing our children physically, and I
couldn't do this well unless I took the time to really learn about what
she was doing.

My wife has pushed herself in similar ways for my sake. This past
year I became involved in a community musical production of *A
Christmas Carol*. Traditionally, my wife is a more behind-the-scenes/
stagecraft kind of person. But it was my hope that my whole family
could be in the cast, giving our children an opportunity to experience
something that I love and maybe even starting a family Christmas
tradition. My intention, when I started this, was to get some bit part
and hang out in the choir with my family the rest of the time ("It'll be
great honey! We'll be together the whole time!"). What ended up
happening was that I was given two roles (Marley's Ghost and Old
Joe) and was asked to be the musical director as well.

My lovely wife took it all in stride. She attended most of the
rehearsals, even when she didn't have to be there, just so that we would
have some time together as a family. For the first time, she even sang in
public, something she hadn't tried to do since her third-grade music
teacher told her that everyone would be better off if she just lip-
synched. I could imagine that the whole thing—from wrangling our
kids to make sure they were where they needed to be, to doing something in public that she was fairly uncomfortable doing in private—
was no picnic for her. But, through it all, she exhibited grace, courage,
and good humor. I love my wife more than I could ever say, but I can
honestly tell you that I loved her even more after that play because I
treasured the sacrifices her love for me compelled her to make.

My wife and I don't do these things because we don't have our own
lives. The fact is, we enjoy spending time alone and with other people,
and we make giving that time to each other a priority. However, I
would be hard pressed to point to any area of either of our lives in

which the other did not at least have some competency or knowledge. Even when my wife and I do things separately, we can share those experiences because we have made the effort to learn about each other's worlds, and it has made our marriage more fun, more intimate, and more joyful than either of us could have imagined when we started.

Celebrate the Little Things

There are a million and one simple, everyday events to celebrate: Wake up to watch the sunrise together, take the time to savor a favorite meal, make a date to watch your favorite television show (dress for it or serve appetizers and drinks), congratulate your wife for finding the perfect set of earrings to go with that outfit you bought her, make a fuss over the fact that he's wearing your favorite tie. Yes, it's all corny. But corn has always been one of my favorite vegetables.

You could celebrate the anniversary of your first date or first kiss together, and even if you can't remember exactly when this was, simply agree upon a day or celebrate the season of the year it was when you first enjoyed those pleasures with your mate. You could even take a tip from the Rabbit and the Mad Hatter of *Alice's Adventure in Wonderland* and celebrate you or your mate's "un-birthday." (There are 364 of them per year, you know.) Or your might host, on a quarterly basis, that "gratitude party" you read about in the last chapter.

At the very least, I am convinced that every couple needs to make a proper fuss (that is, more than just the traditional dinner and a card) about birthdays, anniversaries, Valentine's Day, and other personal holidays. You don't have to spend a fortune to do this. You just have to show some thoughtfulness and a willingness to be silly. If you like giving cards, then one birthday, make a giant card by painting your message on two four-by-eight-foot sheets of plywood and setting them on the lawn. One anniversary, hide little candy kisses all over the place so that your mate can find them and think of you all day. My wife loves Hostess Ho-Hos, so one Valentine's Day I drew a heart and wrote "I love you" by taping the contents of about three boxes of individually wrapped Ho-Hos to two sheets of posterboard. If you want your love for your mate to feel big, you can't be afraid of occasionally showing it, telling it, and demonstrating it in a big way.

Humor

Exceptional Joy also manifests itself in the healthy sense of humor the Exceptional couple has about themselves, each other, their relationship, and life in general. Life is not one big sitcom for Exceptional couples ("This happy couple is brought to you by Hallmark Greetings! —when you care enough to wed the very best!") any more than it is for you. But Exceptional couples work to find the fun where they can.

Maria especially loves her husband's ability to make her laugh when she's stressed. "Sometimes, when I am totally fried, he'll put his arms around me and start singing that Monty Python Song, 'Always Look on the Bright Side of Life' in a hackneyed Russian accent. It's the stupidest thing in the world, but I laugh every time."

A good sense of humor is a sign of mental health. The *Diagnostic and Statistical Manual* (fourth edition) of the American Psychiatric Association (a book that is every bit as fun as it sounds) describes its Defensive Functioning Scale, which rates all the various "defense mechanisms" (that is, ways that people mentally guard themselves from being overwhelmed by stress) from least to most healthy. In the healthiest category, listed with other high-level defense mechanisms (for example, proactivity, self-awareness, altruism, help-seeking), is a sense of humor.

Humor gives perspective and bonds people together. It lowers a couple's emotional temperature (see chapter 8) so that they can find solutions which are less obvious to a person under stress. When you laugh with your mate, you are reminded that even in terms of stress you are teammates. Somehow, even the simplest, well-timed joke can stop a couple from reenacting their favorite scenes from *The Exorcist* when what they really need to be doing is having a healthy problem-solving session.

A sense of humor is one of those things that people think you either have or you don't. But this isn't true. For example, comedian Drew Carey, in an interview on NPR's *Fresh Air,* said that he didn't know how to write a joke until he read a self-help book that described how to be funny. At first I thought he was kidding, but he assured the interviewer several times that he was quite serious. The fact is, almost anyone can improve both their sense of humor and their appropriate use of that humor in marriage.

The best kind of humor in marriage supports and strengthens the couple. It is perfectly fine to make fun of your situation or even, at times, yourself. It is rarely, if ever, appropriate to make fun of your mate. Granted, there is some element of teasing that is part and parcel of any marriage, but sometimes even the most innocent joke at our mate's expense can seriously damage a relationship.

I recently counseled a woman whose primary complaint was that she felt repulsed by the idea of making love with her husband. When tracking back to see where this originated, my client said that about five years previous, her husband saw her getting out of the shower, said, "Hey, chubby," and then gave her a hug. "Ever since then," she said, "I can't stand being naked around him. I don't want him touching me. He's said over and over that it was all a joke. But I just can't get it out of my mind. How can I trust someone who can be so mean to me?"

The husband then made matters worse by accusing her of over-reacting and being oversensitive. He kept repeating that any problem she had with the situation was her problem because, after all, he was, "only kidding." Of course, she took this to mean that he was trying to get out of having called her fat, by now calling her crazy.

Later, when I was talking with the husband the poor, misguided SOB said, "She got it all wrong. She was complaining all day about how fat she was. And truthfully, she had put on a few pounds, but I didn't care. I was only trying to show her that I loved her no matter what she weighed."

Obviously, I had some work to do here. Between how grossly this couple had miscalculated each other's reactions and how poorly they communicated their intentions to each other, it was clear that this couple's lack of rapport existed long before the regrettable shower incident. The amount of rapport in a marriage ultimately determines how much teasing a couple can tolerate. It is decidedly easier to choke down a joke at your own expense if you know that the teller of the joke is, most of the time, a fierce guardian of your dignity and an affectionate, grateful partner. If you can honestly say that you are living the five-to-one rule, that you and your mate are five times more loving, affectionate, and playful in a positive way than you are critical or "joking" in a negative way, then your marriage can probably tolerate a small amount of teasing. But again, you must be careful with negative humor because what is intended as an affectionate slap on the behind by one spouse might just as easily be interpreted as demeaning, or even abusive, by the other.

If a good sense of humor benefits a couple when things are going well, it is doubly beneficial when that same couple is under stress or in conflict, but these are understandably the worst times to try to develop your effervescent wit. Using humor to diffuse stress is only possible to the degree that you and your mate regularly laugh together when things are going well. That is why an Exceptional couple works to make their house a "fun house."

For some people, a positive and uplifting sense of humor is a natural gift. And then there are others, like myself, who seem to have inherited a gene for curmudgeonliness and have to work a little harder. Either way, filling your house with laughter can be as simple as doing the unexpected romantic thing (like standing on the lawn below your bedroom window and serenading your lover—especially if you can't sing), breaking into spontaneous silliness (like grabbing your mate and dancing your version of the hustle just to be a pest), or making frequent trips to the humor section of your local book store. I have been told that the first rule of comedy is, "If you can't make your own funny, steal someone else's." Help yourself to the humorously skewed visions of people like Dave Barry, Bill Cosby, Dennis Miller, Bill Maher, and others like them. (Paul Rieser does a dead-on funny treatment of marriage and family life in his two books, *Couplehood* and *Babyhood,* and Loretta LaRoache is a motivational speaker who, both in person and in her book *Relax!,* does a very funny job of showing how humor can help you get out of your own way and get what you want out of life.)

Likewise, you can watch some humorous videos with your mate, go to comedy clubs, or read the books I have recommended above aloud with your mate. By apprenticing with the masters, you can begin to learn how to use your own sense of humor as a powerful weapon for beating off the stress gremlins whose greatest pleasure is stealing the joy from your life and marriage.

Exceptional Joy: An Exercise

Sharing Interests

You and your mate may have some hobbies, pursuits, or other areas of interest which you do not share. Each one of these things is another opportunity to capitalize on the intimacy and playfulness in your marriage.

A husband and wife do not need to do everything together all of the time. However, having at least some competence, interest, and involvement in these separate areas will increase the amount of intimacy and joy in your marriage. Examine and discuss these areas to see if you are missing out on opportunities to demonstrate your love to each other and reap the benefits of Exceptional Joy.

- Think about a time in your life when you pushed yourself to try something, for your mate's sake, and it turned out well. How did this experience make you feel about yourself, your mate, and your marriage?
- What interests, hobbies, or passions do you and your mate *not* share?
- What could you do to become at least a little bit more competent or involved in these areas?
- How would your relationship benefit from a greater degree of sharing in these areas?
- What obstacles would you see to sharing these areas of your lives and how could you overcome them?
- Grab a pencil and paper and list ten simple things you have always wanted to do, learn, or try, but have not experienced as of this date (for example, take a hot air balloon ride, learn Asian massage techniques, take a turkey-calling class, eat alligator meat, learn to knit couch covers, whatever—the more unusual the better).

Make plans to do these things—*together!* When possible, mark them on your calendar. Spread them out over the course of the year so that you and your mate will have plenty of new experiences to share in the coming months.

Celebrating the Little Things

- Think of two or three recent occasions when you and your mate had a particularly good time together. What was so meaningful about these events? When could you do them again? Make some plans today.
- Get your calendar. Mark down as many relationship "firsts" as you and your mate can recall (examples include, first date, first kiss, when you proposed). Make plans to mark these occasions with some small celebration of your love.
- Celebrate the blessings you have by giving something back to your

community as a couple—volunteer at a soup kitchen, build a house with Habitat for Humanity, visit the sick or elderly.

Improving Your Sense of Humor

- When was the last time you and your mate shared a laugh together? What could the two of you do to have more moments like these?
- Are you comfortable with the amount of teasing that goes on in your marriage? If not, identify some of the sensitive topics. Right now, make a pledge not to joke about these issues, especially in an argument. Discuss how you could talk about these subjects in a way that would not be offensive to either of you.
- How good are you at laughing at yourself? Do you take things too personally? What can you do to be better at taking your shortcomings in stride—even as you work to overcome them?
- Make a date to do something silly or out of the ordinary. Have a picnic on the living room floor, host a murder mystery party, sign yourselves up for a game of paintball, play a new board game, make love outdoors, go to a karaoke club, read a comedy book together—use your imagination. Don't be afraid to be as outrageous as you want to be.

In the film *As Good as It Gets,* Jack Nicholson walks out of his therapist's office and into the patient-filled waiting room. He fixes his angry gaze at the overtly angst-ridden group and says, "What if this is as good as it gets?"

There is a great temptation to think that joy is just around the corner. If we could only possess that object, acquire that position, solve that problem, then we could finally relax, we could finally enjoy ourselves. I, myself, fall prey to this line of thinking on many occasions. But this is it, folks. This is life. And whether it is as good as it gets or not depends a great deal on your willingness to look for the joy hidden in the simple, everyday things: the love in your partner's eyes; the way she makes you happy to have lungs just so that you can breathe the same air as her; the way he makes you smile when you should be crying. These are all ways joy reveals itself in the present moments. Stop looking elsewhere for what you already have and let joy rule your day.

11

Exceptional Sexuality

The wise know that physical pleasure is not the sole end of lovemaking. It can be like music,... dissolving thoughts into rhythm... till that music itself breaks into one, long, holy note of silence.

—KAMA SUTRA

NINETY-FIVE PERCENT of great sex is in the mind, and with Exceptional Joy on their minds, it's no wonder that Exceptional couples enjoy an outstandingly sensual, soulful love life. This chapter will explore the steps you must take to create a deeply spiritual, highly sensual, Exceptional Sexuality.

In order to understand where the underlying beliefs of Exceptional Sex originate, and to help you exhibit those attitudes in your own marriage, I am going to walk you through the five stages of sexual attitudes. Every person does not need to go through all of these stages, but just as with the Relationship Pathway (page 24), once you have found your starting place on the Sexuality Continuum, you will tend to proceed through the following stages in order.

Your growth toward Exceptional Sexuality reflects all the traits of

The Sexuality Continuum

The Sexuality Continuum represents the evolution of sexual attitudes. As a couple matures through the continuum, they learn to effectively integrate the physical, psycho-social, and spiritual aspects of their personhood into their lovemaking.

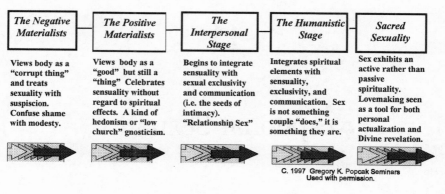

The Negative Materialists	The Positive Materialists	The Interpersonal Stage	The Humanistic Stage	Sacred Sexuality
Views body as a "corrupt thing" and treats sexuality with suspiscion. Confuse shame with modesty.	Views body as a "good" but still a "thing" Celebrates sensuality without regard to spiritual effects. A kind of hedonism or "low church" gnosticism.	Begins to integrate sensuality with sexual exclusivity and communication (i.e. the seeds of intimacy). "Relationship Sex"	Integrates spiritual elements with sensuality, exclusivity, and communication. Sex is not something couple "does," it is something they are.	Sex exhibits an active rather than passive spirituality. Lovemaking seen as a tool for both personal actualization and Divine revelation.

C. 1997 Gregory K. Popcak Seminars
Used with permission.

Figure 11.1

the Exceptional person: greater personal competence, more internalized boundaries, and a more positive view of yourself and the world. Most remarkably, as a couple moves along the Sexuality Continuum (Figure 11.1), they begin to integrate their spirituality, values, ideals, and goals into their sex lives in ways that exponentially increase the joyful, orgasmic power of their lovemaking.

The first two stages on the Sexuality Continuum, Negative Materialism and Positive Materialism, are most common in the Impoverished marriage group.

Stage One: The Negative Materialists ("Aunt McGillicuddy's Antique Urn School")

"I don't ever want him to touch me again," said Jacqueline of her husband. "The other day, I caught him watching that *Baywatch* show. I can't believe the immodesty that's allowed on television. Of course I made him turn it off. But worse still, that night he wanted to have sex! How could he possibly think that I would want to be with him after he spent half the night ogling other women? I'm not going to let myself be used that way."

My pet name for the Negative Materialists is "Aunt McGillicuddy's Antique Urn School" of human sexuality. Rather than using the power of their sexuality in good, true, and beautiful ways, they fear it, approaching lovemaking delicately, cautiously, and, ideally, infrequently, like Aunt McGillicuddy's Antique Urn: "Don't ye be fussin' with *that* now, missy! We only touch it if we have to dust it. And then only once a month or so!"

Negative Materialists focus on the body as a thing (and an undesirable thing at that) which has no spiritual usefulness. (This is ironic, because people in this category tend to highjack religious ideas to justify their pathology.) In fact, in the opinion of people in this group, the body is something that is so corrupted that it is best viewed as an enemy. Negative Materialists have a very shame-based view of sexuality and confuse modesty with shame. Modesty is a necessary virtue—a part of healthy boundary setting—that protects the intimate core of a person, but shame is a vice which prevents an individual from sharing that intimate core with the person for whom it is intended, most specifically, a husband or wife.

The Aunt McGillicuddy view is most often held by people who have some emotional trauma in their history or who were raised in a severely punitive environment. Because sex is viewed as something that is dangerous, and potentially victimizing, the Negative Materialist is usually a very cautious, fearful lover who gets little personal pleasure from most kinds of physical intimacy. Paradoxically, however, some Negative Materialists may develop an unhealthy and potentially illicit obsession with sex, due their constant attempts to deny the sexual aspects of their humanity. Many so-called "sex addicts" fall into this latter category.

Stage Two: The Positive Materialists ("The Madonna School")

"We've always had a pretty adventurous sex life," said Gary. "Rhonda has never shied away from anything. We've used lots of different toys and had a lot of pretty wild experiences. Once or twice we've even gotten together with some married friends of ours and traded partners. Like I said, things have always been good. But lately, Rhonda hasn't been herself. She's pushing me away. We used to have sex at least every day—sometimes two or three times. Now, she acts like she doesn't want anything to do with me. I don't know what the hell she wants."

Like the McGillicuddy-ites before them, Positive Materialists also believe that the body is a thing that has little—if any—spiritual value, *but* they believe that sensuality is good and they celebrate it as such. The transformation of pop singer Madonna from the eighties' "Material Girl" to the late nineties' "mystical spiritualist" nicely illustrates the growth of a person through the Positive Materialism stage of human sexuality. Spiritually speaking, Positive Materialists break down into three categories: those who have no spiritual life and merely revel in raw sexuality (that is, hedonists); those who are suspicious of spiritual things because they believe that to be "spiritual" or "religious" you must also be sexually self-punishing; and those who celebrate a kind of "low-church gnosticism" in which the body can do whatever it wants as long as the mind occupies itself with "mystical things." Many Positive Materialists are former alums of the Aunt McGillicuddy school who broke free of the obsessive-compulsive trap of Negative Materialism by asserting the goodness of the physical sensations of sexuality.

To be fair, this position represents the very beginning of seeing the body—and the human person—as a good thing. But Positive Materialism is still a fairly shallow philosophy of sex. It inhibits true intimacy by placing "exciting sensations" over meaningful relationships and confusing mere copulation with real love. Many married couples I have counseled at this stage have little understanding—if they have any at all—of how to be friends to each other, but believe their relationship to be secure because, as Gary said in the example above, "we have sex almost every day—sometimes two or three times."

Positive Materialists can't rely on the fire of their intimacy to enliven their lovemaking so they tend to be extremely dependent on kinky sex toys or "exotic" sexual practices like "swinging" or milder forms of sadomasochistic sex to keep things "interesting." Though a couple finds the novelty of such experiences fun at first, these same experiences eventually undermine the spiritual core of a marriage. The great irony is that most of these couples aren't even conscious of the spiritual core of their marriage, but as it begins rotting, a wife may complain that she no longer feels "special" to her husband and begin to see herself as "just another way my husband relieves himself." For his part, a husband who starts out as a gung-ho Positive Materialist ("Come on, honey, have sex with other men while I watch, it'll be great!") may eventually come to mourn the loss of a wife who "accidentally" fell in love with a sex partner she had while the couple was "swinging." Or he may complain that his wife "would rather spend time with her vibrator than she would with me."

In every good lie there is a grain of truth. Couples are right to celebrate the goodness of their sensuality and to engage in free and pleasurable sexual play with each other. But when human sexuality is reduced to mere eroticism, it is only a matter of time before self-esteem suffers and relationships collapse.

Stage Three: The Interpersonal Stage (When "Relationship Sex" Starts to Look Good)

The next stage, the Interpersonal Stage, represents the sexual attitudes held by most Conventional/Apprentice couples.

"Jerry and I have a good sex life," says Theresa of her relationship with her husband of nine years. "We always try to find ways to keep both our relationship and our lovemaking fresh and we are very comfortable with each other. If we struggle with anything, it's too little energy and too little time. It's hard to figure out a way to insulate ourselves from all the chaos of our lives, and sometimes that has a negative effect on our sex drives. We certainly don't love each other any less, it's just tough to find the balance."

Couples in the Interpersonal Stage think of lovemaking as "a beautiful and important" thing to do, something that brings two people together. At its best, the Interpersonal Stage serves as the beginning point of meaningful, intimate sex. It helps the husband and wife to set boundaries which protect their dignity, prevents them from treating each other as objects, and still allows the couple to enjoy a pleasurable and somewhat varied sex life within those boundaries.

There tend to be two drawbacks to this stage. The first is that an undesirable side effect of healthy boundary-setting is often the politicization of sexual relations. Just as marital chicken and domestic scorekeeping are played in other parts of the Conventional couple's marriage, it can be played in the bedroom too. For example, a couple may have arguments over certain sexual acts which make one partner feel "less equal" than the other. Oral sex and rear-entry positions are two fairly common examples of this. Or, a couple may argue about how much sex is a "fair" amount when a husband and wife have differing ideas about the frequency of lovemaking.

The temptation for many Conventional couples is to deal with these problems as sexual issues. But trying to solve these problems head-on will only make them worse because they are not primarily sexual problems, they are sexual manifestations of the ways Conventional couples relate to each other in all aspects of their relationship. The only way to completely resolve these "sexual problems" is for the couple to pursue egalitarianism over equity, competence over "being taken care of," and a greater attitude of service over a fear of being taken advantage of—in general. Without taking this frightening step, both the marriage and, in turn, the sexual relationship will stagnate.

The second difficulty of this stage is that since lovemaking is merely an important thing to do (albeit a pleasant thing) it tends to be placed at the bottom of the pile of other important things to do. Conventional/Apprentice couples are very busy people. Their primary focus on gaining approval from employers, parents, friends, committees, and organizations makes them insensitive to their need to nurture their psychological and relational health. In turn, the exhaustion and stress resulting from such hectic lives either kills or greatly diminishes sexual desire, making Inhibited Sexual Desire Disorder (ISDD) one of the fastest growing clinical problems in married America.

If the conventional couple isn't careful to nurture their psychological and relationship health, what was once warm, safe, pleasurable "relationship sex" can quickly turn into frustrating, "I'm too tired for" sex. But if both the husband and wife do the work required in all aspects of their relationship, the couple can move to the next stage of sexual development, the Humanistic Stage.

Stage Four: The Humanistic Stage
("Sex Is Not Something We Do, It's Something We Are")

The Humanistic Stage tends to correspond with high-end Conventional marriages and beginning Exceptional Partnership marriages.

Deborah and Phillip, married twenty-two years, have active lives and are the parents of four children. Even so, they share what they describe as a fabulous sex life. "I don't understand my friends who tell me that their lovemaking is either flat or nonexistent," says Deborah. "Maybe we're just lucky, but the spark Phillip and I had at the start of our relationship is still there. In fact, it's more like lightning now. We know each other so well and have been through so much together, I don't see how the spark couldn't have grown. There is no one on earth who would know how to please me half as well as Phillip—in or out of bed." She gave a coy smile. "And I *know* he'd say the same about me."

At the Humanistic Stage, the couple is aware of the intimate connection between Exceptional Service in all aspects of the marriage and great sex in the bedroom (or any other room for that matter). The couple understands—on an experiential level (rather than merely an intellectual level like many Conventional couples)—that sex is a language spoken by one body and soul to another. While sex to less exceptional couples represents something they *do,* sex for these couples is something they *are.* Lovemaking is seen as the most profound expression of the mutual service the couple gives to each other all day, every day. It is as if, through lovemaking, the husband and wife say to each other, "Look how well we love one another, even our bodies work for each other's good!"

Practically speaking, this results in the politics and scorekeeping being removed from the bedroom (it has also been excised from the marriage in general). Because this couple's personal, dignity-protecting boundaries are now being internalized, they no longer require as many external rules (like marital chicken and emotional scorekeeping) to protect their integrity. As long as a sexual act respects the exclusivity of the bond and does not violate the couple's moral integrity it will be acceptable to both the husband and wife—and enjoyed thoroughly.

Likewise, while more Conventional couples tend to lose lovemaking in the list of other "things" they have to do, the Humanistic couple would never think of neglecting their sexual relationship. For them, to make love is to reenact their marriage ceremony, to physically renew their wedding vows, and to celebrate a ritual that symbolizes everything they are to each other. This couple does not view lovemaking as an energy-draining performance, or another "nice thing to do" that, unfortunately, they no longer have the time for, but as a life-giving reality in which they assert both the strength of their bond and the depth of their mutual, generous service, and from which they draw strength to deal with those aspects of their lives (like work and social commitments) which are less fascinating than their relationship.

The Humanistic couple seeks to give as much priority and respect to their sex lives as they did to their wedding day. For example, almost every wedding is the result of months of exhausting preparation (since at least the late Paleozoic Era) and when the wedding day comes, most brides and grooms tend to be exhausted—emotionally and physically—from all of their labors. But, remarkably, in spite of all the exhaustion, no bride or groom ever calls his or her intended the day of the wedding and says, "You know, Honey. I just don't have it in me to get married today. I'm just too darned tired to go to the ceremony. Let's put it off until I get some more rest/finish that stressful project at work/etc., okay?"

A wedding might be postponed for some catastrophe, but it would never be delayed simply because the couple was "too tired" or "too stressed" to bother with it today.

Granted, Exceptional Sex is not always acrobatic, especially when the couple is tired or stressed. But for this couple, lovemaking is an intentional expression of the deep friendship and intimacy they share. In light of this, sometimes an Exceptional husband or wife may make love even when they are not initially physically desirous, because expressing desire is less important than expressing true love (their willingness to work for the good of each other). In sum, lovemaking at the Humanistic Stage and beyond is a wedding banquet which both husband and wife feel privileged to attend regardless of their present physical or emotional state. It is a symbol of all the good things they represent to each other, and it is a reenactment of their promise to love one another in sickness and health, wealth and poverty, good times and bad, stress or no stress, sleep or no sleep, from this day forward, until death do them part.

It is curious then, that some couples, as they approach the Humanistic Stage, encounter what Dr. Schwartz in *Peer Marriage* refers to as an "incest taboo" to lovemaking. In essence, the couple's relationship advances to the point where day-to-day life is so good, the marital friendship is so deep, and the couple is so intimate that—counterintuitively—sex no longer seems an appropriate way for them to relate to each other. Dr. Schwartz merely describes this phenomenon and offers no explanation for it, but since this "incest taboo" is not universally experienced by couples approaching Exceptional couplehood, I believe that the determining factor is the attitude the couple had about sex to begin with.

For all our claims to be a sexually liberated society, most people still think of sex in negative terms. People talk about having sex as "being bad" or "getting nasty." But as a husband and wife approach Exceptional couplehood, there is little that is bad about themselves or their relationship, so the negative connotation of "being bad" no longer applies. In other words, since the couple gets along so well and there is no reason to ever "be nasty" toward each other, there is likewise no longer any congruent way to "get nasty" with each other. Dr. Schwartz observes that some couples try to get around this by giving themselves permission to pretend to "be bad" when it comes to their sex lives. But this is patently unhealthy from a psychological perspective because it uses a defense mechanism called "compart-mentalization" or "splitting" (that is, the person acts one way in one context and another way in a different context and never the twain shall meet). This defense mechanism falls under the "major image distorting" category (read, "damn unhealthy") on the Defensive Functioning Scale I mentioned in the last chapter.

The only psychologically congruent way to resolve the so-called "incest taboo" is to see that sex was never the problem, only the metaphor the person was using for sex was problematic. Eroticism (that is, sex cut loose from true, working-for-the-good-of-each-other love) can be "bad" or "dirty" because it stimulates the body without respect for the soul, but eroticism and Exceptional Sex are two completely different things. The most powerful forms of marital sexuality, what I call Exceptional Sex, are never "bad" or "dirty," because while they involve intensely erotic elements, they also enable the couple to honor the god that dwells within each partner.

Stage Five: Sacred Sex
("Lovemaking As a Spiritually Active Way to Connect With the Divine")

The final stage, Sacred Sex, is practiced by couples at the high end of the Partnership marriage category and by Romantic Peers.

"For us," says George, "sex is a kind of prayer. When we make love, Veronica and I not only work to give ourselves to each other, but we try to use our lovemaking as a way to understand how God is reaching out to each one of us." Veronica agrees: "Looking at our physical relationship this way has added a whole new dimension. Things were

always good between us. But now, it's unbelievable. I don't know
exactly how to put it, except to say that it's like the difference between
singing a song, and becoming the song."

The *Janus Report on Sexual Behavior* (1993) states that spiritual
people have more satisfying sex lives because they "pay more
attention to the mystic and symbolic dimensions of one's sexuality."
Here, you will see why this is true. Sacred sex distinguishes itself from
all the other stages by two remarkable qualities: lovemaking as an
experience of God and lovemaking as a path to personal growth.

Lovemaking as an Experience of God

Other couples may instinctively cry out, "Oh my God!" at the height
of passion, but couples practicing sacred sex know why. Lovemaking
is a religious experience and not just metaphorically speaking.
Beyond simply honoring the god that dwells in each of us, as
Humanistic couples do, the highest level of Exceptional Sexuality
emboldens a couple to understand how God himself relates to us
through our sexuality. (It's not for nothing that saints, mystics, gurus,
and all forms of spiritual masters have compared being in the Divine
Presence to being in ecstasy.) The specific ways a couple experiences
this revelation may differ slightly depending upon their understanding of God and their faith tradition, but all couples practicing Sacred
Sex know that God is there and that He is revealing himself in a
powerful way.

The author Deepak Chopra once posed the serious question,
"Does God have orgasms?" I, like Chopra, believe the answer is
"Absolutely yes." My own faith tradition teaches that God is a lover
and that the cosmological orgasm physicists refer to as the Big Bang,
through which the Universe was created and from which the Universe
continues to reel even today, is the model for human sexuality. Who
wouldn't give their eye tooth for a night like that with their beloved?

C. S. Lewis once wrote, [God] "lends us a little of His reasoning
powers and that is how we think: He puts a little of His love into us
and that is how we love one another." The same is true of our
sexuality. God enjoys his own "sexuality" and because he is generous,
he shares that sexuality with us. Some of you are probably appalled by
what must seem to be a hopeless anthropomorphism on my part. But
when I refer to God's "sexuality" or even God's "orgasms" I don't

mean it in the physical way we humans understand it. Rather, God's "sexuality" is expressed in his joy in loving all things, uniting all things, and creating all things. What we mortals refer to as our sexuality is the power God lends us to join him in loving, uniting, and creating both on a physical level (through lovemaking which leads to children) and on a spiritual level (through lovemaking which strengthens the unity of the couple and actualizes their values, ideals, and goals).

The most exceptional lovers understand this, and as a result, they experience their lovemaking not only as self-revelation, but as Divine Revelation.

Lovemaking as a Path to Personal Growth

Like the Humanistic couples before them, those husbands and wives who practice sacred sex see lovemaking as a physical expression of all that is good in their marriage. But even more importantly, they understand their sexuality as a powerful tool that can be used to pursue personal growth and actualization.

The deepest levels of emotional, relational, and spiritual growth require a person to embrace vulnerability: the willingness to have one's weaknesses exposed so that one can be made whole. There are few instances in life when a person is more vulnerable than when he or she is making love with his or her soul mate. This vulnerability can be intimidation for more conventional couples who protect themselves from it by playing various forms of marital chicken and emotional scorekeeping. Exceptional couples, on the other hand, are exhilarated by the vulnerability they experience in the arms of their beloved because they understand the healing and transformative power that accompanies loving vulnerably. Allow me to offer you a lovely example of this.

Christianne is the mother of five children, each by cesarean section. The scars on her abdomen made her extremely self-conscious, especially during lovemaking, but initially, she was too embarrassed to share this with her husband. When she finally confessed the shame she felt over her appearance, her husband said with—she told me—unmistakable sincerity, "You are so beautiful. Each one of those marks is a gift, given to me by a woman who loves me enough to bear my children."

Any woman who has ever borne children will understand how deeply that man's words touched his wife. By exposing herself fully, body and soul, to her husband's love, she learned not only to accept her appearance, but to celebrate it. The very scars she once saw as a disfigurement are now experienced by her as "marks of honor" (her words) which tell the story of her and her husband's life-giving love.

Sex has an immense power to challenge every emotional, relational, and spiritual boundary a person has. To rise to these challenges with grace, dignity, and even passion is the goal and privelege of the Exceptional couple practicing sacred sex.

Of course, there is a spiritual—perhaps even eternal—benefit to embracing the vulnerability experienced through exceptional love-making. When I die, I believe that I am going to stand before my Divine Lover and all his glory—in all my glory (so to speak). Every blemish, wrinkle, crease, and bump of my physical and spiritual being will be exposed to his penetrating gaze, completely vulnerable to his all-pervasive touch—for all eternity. Under such circumstances, for me to experience anything other than the sheer terror of Hell, I must be able to stand confidently in the presence of that gaze. What better way to prepare myself for this awesome responsibility than to challenge whatever vulnerability or shame I may feel when my wife gazes upon me in my nakedness and makes love with me? It is this unique power of sexuality to challenge shame and expand vulnerability at the deepest level of our personhood that makes lovemaking a spiritual exercise, first and foremost.

Exceptional Sex: Your Master Class

To fully immerse themselves in all the benefits Exceptional Sexuality brings to marriage, some Exceptional couples make use of what I call "creative abstinence" in their love lives. Creative abstinence is best understood as the conscious effort a couple makes to enflame their desire for one another and enhance their intimacy by taking short breaks (about a week or so) from genital intercourse while at the same time intensifying the amount of nongenital physical contact (for example, kissing, cuddling, "making out" without going all the way) and other expressions of affection.

For example, if you and your mate were going to practice creative abstinence for ten days, then on each of those ten days you would make a date with your partner to do any or all of the following: cuddle, make-out without going all the way, play a game or work on a project, go out together, and so on. On the tenth day, while you were cuddling, you might tell each other all the pleasures that you have in store for each other for the following evening. On the eleventh day, and thereafter, you and your mate break your fast, permitting yourselves to feast on the banquet of love you have been planning for days.

Obviously, creative abstinence can be a powerful expression of marital love. It benefits the couple in four major ways. First, it helps them remember the many other ways a couple needs to say "I love you" besides through sexual intercourse. Lovemaking is a wonderful thing, but many couples come to rely on it exclusively as their way of demonstrating affection, forgetting that serving each other throughout the day, cuddling, and other expressions of love can be just as important and just as sweet. Second, when the Exceptional husband or wife both willingly and cheerfully surrender their sexual claims to each other—even if only for a short period of time each month—it allows them to see that, more than mere gratification, the relationship is the essential center of their sexuality. By enhancing respect for each partner and for the strength of the marriage, the couple leaves little room for either mate to ever—even fleetingly— feel used or taken for granted by their lover. Third, suspending lovemaking for a time requires the couple to communicate and solve conflicts rather than merely "sexing" their way through problems, as all couples are wont to do at one time or another (especially the Materialists). Sex therapists and marriage counselors are well aware of this phenomenon and regularly prescribe some form of creative abstinence to help clients recalibrate their relationships. Finally, and most importantly, periodic abstinence has the potential to raise lovemaking to a high art form and means to actualization.

Think about it. Great painters are celebrated as much for their "use of space" as they are for their ability to fill up a canvas with meaningful shapes, colors, and images. Great composers are praised equally for their use of sound and their use of silence to evoke certain moods through their music. In the same way, truly great lovers know how to use both tension and release to experience the full force of a passion that is uniquely spiritual, uniquely sensual, and uniquely theirs.

Creative abstinence has been praised in periodicals as diverse as the pop culture chronicler *Notorious* and the mainstream women's magazine *Redbook*. Thomas Moore devotes a whole section of his book *The Soul of Sex* to "The Joy of Celibacy" in marriage. And little wonder. Besides raising lovemaking to a high art form, creative abstinence is a means to actualization because it allows the couple to practice all their virtues—one set at a time. When they are making love, they can become more generous, passionate, open, vulnerable, expressive, and so on, and when they are not making love they can become more temperate, patient, self-controlled, sensitive, wise, caring, serving, and so on. Yes, of course, other couples can develop all of their virtues even if they don't practice creative abstinence, but taking a short timeout from lovemaking each month allows a couple to focus on certain qualities exclusively, like the sculptor who says, "Today I am going to intimately concentrate on the details of my model's hands." It is this sense of detail—craftsmanship, if you will— that allows Exceptional couples to be masters of the sexual arts. Indeed, masters of the art of life in general.

The Exceptional couple does not think of lovemaking as "the thing we do when we're naked," but rather, "the way we celebrate our relationship all day long." Exceptional Lovemaking is as much social intercourse (see chapter 6) as it is physical intercourse. Exceptional couples know how to feel as close to each other painting a room together as they do lying in each other's arms. This doesn't mean that Exceptional Sex is as exciting as watching paint dry. It means that every time an Exceptional couple works side by side, they experience an intense sexual charge. While lovemaking is the most exalted form of communicating their love for each other, the Exceptional couple knows that the "words" their bodies speak to one another in love-making will be empty and meaningless unless they can refer back to the mutual service, outstanding rapport, and intense desire they share all day long. While other couples roll over in bed and say, out of the blue, "You wanna do it?" Exceptional couples have been engaging in extended foreplay all day through social intercourse and frequent, intense, passionate, spiritual lovemaking is the spontaneous, logical result.

The Seven Paths to Exceptional Sex

Consider this your invitation to the greatest sexual experience of your life. Follow the Seven Paths to Exceptional Sex and you will experience a passion so intense that it will melt your defenses, set your hearts ablaze, and forge your souls into one.

The First Path: Guard Each Other's Dignity

Exceptional lovers are passionate guardians of each other's dignity. They would just as soon cut out their own tongues as intentionally belittle their mate (especially when they are "just kidding"). And they would go to almost any length to avoid using their mate as a mere sexual object.

Exceptional Sexuality cannot exist in the face of cruel humor, blunt criticism, name-calling, neglect (benign or malignant), abuse, or other affronts to one's personal dignity. It also cannot exist as long as either of you has any sense that you are being used by your mate as a mere object for their gratification.

Earlier in this book, I shared the importance maintaining the five-to-one rule in your marriage—the idea that you must be five times more affectionate, generous, complimentary, thoughtful, and kind than critical, nagging, arguing, nitpicking, or contemptuous. But it has been both my professional and personal experience that this five-to-one ratio is only the beginning point of Exceptional Sexuality, which usually does not flourish until a couple has achieved a positivity to negativity ratio of seven to one, or even ten to one.

If you want to celebrate Exceptional Sexuality in your marriage, then the only answer is to love. Love more, love better, love every day. Love by doing the little things. Love in a way that is meaningful to your mate, not necessarily because they deserve it, but because your own dignity demands it.

The Second Path: Be a Servant

Exceptional Service is the second path to Exceptional Lovemaking. Too often, couples try to whine their way into a more fulfilling sexual or romantic life, saying things like, "When are you going to make time for me?" "Do you know how long its been since we had sex?" or "You never take me out anywhere! How come you're not more like so and so?"

Any romance or sex resulting from such pathetic "interventions" will be born of guilt, will not be remarkably satisfying for anyone involved, and will be deeply resented by all concerned—probably for a very long time.

The only way to truly develop the love life you want is to walk the second path and become a servant (see chapter 6). Sex will only evolve into the mutual self-gift it is supposed to be when both you and your mate become equally skilled at serving one another charitably, generously, and joyfully outside of the bedroom. To better understand what I mean, take the following quiz.

OBSTACLES TO EXCEPTIONAL SEX

You and your mate should take this quiz separately. Answer yes or no to each of the following items.

1. Instead of engaging in a mutual pursuit of competence, do you keep score of the amount of effort you are both putting into the upkeep of the house and marriage, making certain it is fifty-fifty at all times?

2. Do you ever belittle your mate (even when you are "just kidding")? Do you discourage the pursuit of his or her dreams, goals, values, interests, or ideas?

3. Do you pout, or act disgusted or uninterested when accompanying your mate to some place or function that is meaningful to him or her but not to you (for example, shopping, visiting in-laws, attending corporate functions, church, hobbies)?

4. Do you use your marriage as an institution of convenience saying, "Now that I'm married I never have to do X again. That's what my spouse is for."?

5. Do you refuse or resist loving your mate in a way that is meaningful to him or her?

6. Are you afraid of what having children would do to you or your marriage? Or if you have children, do you leave most of the parenting to your spouse?

7. Do you consistently give more time and energy to your family of origin, work, social roles, hobbies, or other interests than you do your marriage and family?

8. Do you refuse or resist doing things your mate asks you to do, not because those things violate your morals, but because you "just don't feel like it"?

9. Do you tend to do loving things for your mate and then become resentful if you are not rewarded in kind?

10. Do you or your mate leave arguments feeling beaten up?

11. Do your arguments end with no mutually satisfactory solution in sight?

12. Do you tend to do loving things only when you want something from your mate? Do you tend to be more loving than usual when you want something from your mate?

Each yes answer represents another way you are indirectly undermining the sexual potential of your marriage. The only way to achieve Exceptional Sex is to invite it by working to become a better lover outside the bedroom. And don't think you can trick your mate by "serving them" with the intention of being "paid" with more or "better" sex. You must serve for the sake of service—for the sake of your marital imperative—itself. When you do this, to the degree that your mate needs you to do it, Exceptional Sexuality will blossom all on its own, because a vital sexuality is the logical, loving response to joyfully given marital service.

The Third Path: Approach Lovemaking Joyfully

Sex is not a chore, an extra, or even a "nice thing" to do when you have the energy. Exceptional Sex is not something you do, it is something you are. Exceptional Sex is the joyful renewal of your wedding vows. It is the celebration that accompanies loving and serving each other so well that even your bodies work for each other's good. It is the manifestation of your power to love, unite, and create. Exceptional Sex is not a performance that saps your strength, it is the well from which you must draw your strength. Exceptional Sex gives couples the freedom to love as passionately, or as quietly, as they need to at any given time. It also gives couples the freedom to willingly and cheerfully put aside genital expressions of love for a time so that they can rejoice in the other aspects of their relationship and life, which are just as important and just as sweet.

The Fourth Path: Love Vulnerably

If you and your mate are pursuing your marital imperative, fiercely guarding each other's dignity, and attempting to practice the many forms of Exceptional Service in your marriage, then it is time to let the emotional and physical barriers to intimacy come down. Love vulnerably.

Give your mate the gift of your whole self. If you are ashamed of your body or your sexuality in any way, gradually work toward giving your mate the gift of experiencing and loving your body for all that it is by loving in all the senses (see chapter 7). Make love with the lights on. No, you don't have to make love under a halogen lamp, but let your lover see you. Kiss with your eyes open, or do what Dr. David Schnarch recommends in his book *Passionate Marriage:* The next time you are making love, look directly into your mate's eyes as you climax—look directly into your lover's soul.

Besides these visual opportunities for exposing your vulnerabilities, there are auditory and kinesthetic ones as well. The next time you are making love, tell your mate the things you most want them to know while you are making love with them. Say, "I love how you are touching me now" or "I love when you touch me there." Or try a variation on this: Don't do anything your mate doesn't specifically tell you to do. Take turns talking each other through exactly what you want, how you want it, and when. Not only does this make both partners feel extremely vulnerable, but it provides an explicitly individualized education of your mate's most intimate likes and dislikes. Whatever you do, compliment your lover. Let your lover know how good he or she is to you and how much you enjoy giving yourself to him or her.

Take turns touching every inch of each other. Make love to every square inch of your mate's body—slowly and intentionally, almost prayerfully. (The rule is, Whatever feels good will feel twice as good half as fast.) Let your partner know how much love every perfect curve, and every imperfect one too. Don't let one single cell be untouched, unkissed, uncarressed. Play, laugh, don't be afraid to be silly. In fact, sometimes, be intentionally silly. Don't be afraid to be sexy. In fact, sometimes, be intentionally sexy—even if that makes you feel or look a little silly. After all, who can be dignified and drunk with love at the same time? If neither silliness nor sexiness comes easy to you, then be glad for one more opportunity to "fake it 'till you make it."

As you experience all these things, you may feel frightened, vulnerable, crazed, passionate, frustrated, and loved, sometimes all at once. But that's where the power of real sex comes from. If you want a truly earth-shattering, mind-bending, soul-shaking sexual experience, put away the sex toys. Try grown-up sex. Try vulnerability.

The Fifth Path: Sometimes, Take Some Time Off

Give your mate the gift of regularly taking a little time off from your lovemaking to concentrate on loving each other in all the other ways that tend to get lost in the shuffle of life. The fourth path was to "love vulnerably" and few things make a person feel more vulnerable than fasting; from sex, from food, from anything. But the vulnerability that comes from fasting bears wonderful fruit.

One thing that people forget is that fasting gives you a ravenous appetite and—when you finally do get to eat again—makes food taste better! Taking a break from lovemaking, even for a short period every month, makes sex that much more special—and orgasms that much more powerful.

The Sixth Path: Embrace the Creative Power of Your Love

Technology has given us the ability to physically separate lovemaking from baby making. But in our minds and bodies, there is an ancient archetype, a code inscribed in every cell of our being that prevents us from separating them entirely. To experience Exceptional Sex, you must know that your mate welcomes every part of you, and our children, the ones we have and the ones we are yet to have, are part of us. When we reject children, either by fearing their conception or being avoidant or unavailable parents, we reject a part of our mate. Eventually, a relationship will suffer from this rejection.

As Peter DeVries put it, "The value of marriage is not that adults produce children, but that children produce adults." Embracing both your potential and actual parenthood allows you to accept the whole gift, the entire package of love that is your mate. Experience children as the sign that your married love is so uniquely powerful that it has to be given its own name.

The Seventh Path: The Lover's Prayer

Earlier, I shared with you some of the spiritual effects of lovemaking: that sex is one way God reaches out to us; that lovemaking is one way to prepare ourselves to spend eternity being intimately and passionately loved by the God who made us. If these ideas appealed to you, you may wish to develop a Lover's Prayer. Mine goes something like this, "Lord, let me kiss her with your lips, love her with your gentle hands, consume her with your undying passion that I may show her how precious and beautiful she is to you."

There are some who think that prayer would have the same effect on lovemaking as reciting baseball statistics, but I have found that this prayer has made me a more patient lover, a more intentional lover, a more gentle, caring, passionate, silly, and more adventurous lover than I might otherwise be. By praying this way, I give my body, mind, and soul to the God who made me, and I become his instrument for loving my wife as well as he wishes her to be loved.

Lovemaking as prayer is far from a somber experience. Prayer comes in many flavors, from the profound ecstasy of the mystic, to the soulful, exuberant joy of a gospel choir, and everything in between. Exceptional Sex can be all of this and more. Thinking of lovemaking as a kind of physical prayer through which God reveals himself to the participants adds a unique and powerful dimension to sex that goes beyond simply honoring the god that dwells within each one of us. It lets the couple know that God himself cares about such a small thing as the pleasure of their love. And it gives both husband and wife an important role to play in the spiritual actualization of one another, by empowering their lovemaking to break down the barriers to intimacy and vulnerability and preparing them to spend eternity in the arms of their Divine Lover.

Was It Good for You?

As this chapter on Exceptional Sex draws to a close, some of you may be tempted to just roll over and go to sleep without doing the discussion questions which follow (isn't that just like a reader? Rushes through the chapter. Never wants to discuss anything...). But I'd encourage you to take some time to sit down with your lover and talk about how to make your lovemaking exceptional.

EXCEPTIONAL SEX: COMING TO A BEDROOM NEAR YOU

You have two options. Either discuss the following questions directly with your mate, or choose a question to write to each other about. After you've exchanged letters and written responses, discuss the experience. Repeat as often as you like.

1. How good is your social intercourse (your ability to communicate and give Exceptional Service to one another)? How do you think this affects your lovemaking? What ways can you improve your partnership out of the bedroom?

2. What do you enjoy most about making love with your partner? When you think of the most fun you ever had making love with your spouse, what springs to mind? What time (or times) was (or were) the most meaningful?

3. Which of the Seven Paths to Exceptional Sex do you already do? What effect has it had on your sex life? What others would you like to add?

4. How do you think shame or fear of vulnerability holds you back as a lover? What can you do to begin overcoming these struggles? How can your mate support you?

5. If you were to "take a short time off" from lovemaking, what areas of your relationship would you like to focus more attention on? How do you think this would benefit you?

Try the following...

1. Make a list of your and your mate's ten most wonderful lovemaking experiences together. Make plans to repeat them.

2. Write your own Lover's Prayer.

3. Take ten consecutive days off from lovemaking this month. Each of the ten days, make a point to give each other loving, focused attention: cuddle together, make out without going all the way, work on a project, go on a date, play a game. On the tenth day, you and your mate should plan all the wonderful things you are going to do break your fast. On the eleventh day (and thereafter), feast!

4. What is the one sexual act, position, or attitude that makes you feel the most vulnerable? Assuming that it does not violate your values, the next time you make love, no matter how scary or silly you feel,

do that thing. The next day, write a letter to your mate telling him or her what it was like to trust them so much. Thank your mate for being worthy of your trust.

5. Some time when you make love, look into each other's eyes as you climax. Don't say a word. Don't make a sound. Instead, focus all your passion through your eyes and into your lover's soul.

6. Some time when you make love, take turns agreeing not to do anything unless your partner tells you what to do, the more specific the better. Have your mate describe what to do, how long to do it, and how fast or slow.

7. Some time when you make love, turn off all the lights. Touch, kiss, and caress your mate's entire body. Use only the movements of his or her body, breath-sounds, and the sounds of his or her pleasure (but no words) to guide you through the entire encounter.

It is my sincere wish and belief that by pursuing all the qualities you have explored in this book, you will become exceptional lovers both in and out of the bedroom. By practicing what you have read, I believe that you will, as Veronica said earlier in the chapter, not only learn to sing love's song, but become the song itself.

Epilogue: Building Your Own
Exceptional Marriage

As we come to the end of our time together, I would like to offer you my gratitude for allowing me to accompany you this far on your marital journey. It is my hope that in each chapter you came away with something you did not have when you started, were reminded of something you used to do but have since forgotten, received some validation for the things you are already doing well in your marriage, and were given some glimpse of the work that still lies ahead of you.

When I talk to couples about Exceptional marriages, I usually get one of three responses. The first is pure disbelief, "Exceptional marriages are too good to be true." But they are not, and research has shown this to be the case. I urge you to resist the temptation to deny the existence of that which you fear you cannot attain, because it *is* attainable. The second response is, "Sure, anyone would love to have a marriage like that, but it's too hard. It's just not realistic for me." Whether this is true or not really depends upon what you decide to build your life around. People make time for what is truly important to them. In the first chapter, you clarified the theme around which you have built your life and marriage. Think about that theme again and ask yourself this question, "Is it enough?" If it is, if you are satisfied, then with all my heart I am happy for you. But if you want more from your life—even if it is already a good life—then I would invite you to respond to this book the way the third group of people do, by saying, "Sign me up. It sounds like a lot of work, but how wonderful!"

Exceptional marriage is hard work. But it is a labor of love because, as you read in chapter 5, love is the labor of marriage. Doing this work enables you and your mate to become "collaborative geniuses"; to not only to have a wonderfully intimate, passionate, and soulful marriage, but also become the people you want to be when you grow up.

When a couple has gotten what they came for out of their counseling experience, I like to spend the last session or two reminding them of what worked best and designing a care plan for their marriage, basically an individually tailored "Owner's Manual" for the care and feeding of their relationship. At this time, I would like to offer you a similar service.

Marriage: An Owner's Manual

Cars, boats, homes, gardens—all have one. In fact, just about every *valuable* thing comes with one. Why don't marriages have maintenance schedules? Most people know how often they have to change their oil, till their garden, rotate their tires, replace their furnace screens, but do you know how often to oil your marriage? Follow the schedule below for a well-maintained relationship.

Every Day

- Say, "I do" every day. Remember, each exchange between you and your mate is another opportunity to affirm or tear down your marriage. For the sake of your relationship and your personal dignity, choose love.
- Ask yourself, "What can I do to make my spouse's life a little easier, more fulfilling, more pleasant today?" Then, do it.
- Find small ways to demonstrate affection. Catch your mate being good. Be generous with kisses, hugs, compliments, and calls from the office.
- Take some time to talk with your mate. Catch up on the news. Solve today's problems. Address issues with the children. Discuss plans for the future.
- Pray. Ask God—*as you understand the concept*—to help you become the lover God would be to your spouse.

Every Week

- Celebrate a family ritual. Have a big meal, even if your family is just the two of you; join a team together. Do anything that will solidify the unique bond that is your marriage and family.

- Are you and your mate getting fifteen hours a week together to talk, work together, and rekindle the romance? What changes do you need to make in your schedule to make sure you get your fifteen hours next week?
- Review your Twenty-five Ways to Make Love—Every Day list (page 90). Are you keeping up? What new loving actions should you add?

Every Month

- Assuming your children are developmentally ready or physically healthy enough, go out as a couple at least once per month. If you can't go out, arrange to have "couple time" at home. Set the kids up with a video, or even have the sitter come to your house, while you and your mate enjoy a piece of pie and grown-up conversation over candlelight in the dining room.

Every Three Months

- Review the chapter on Exceptional Negotiation. How are you doing? What skills do you still need to develop or practice? How, specifically, will you develop those skills?

Every Six Months

- Ask your mate how you could be an even better spouse. Receive any criticism graciously, give criticism kindly, and act on the discussion.
- Read a book on some aspect of marriage /or family life together.

Once a Year

- Go on a retreat together; do a marriage encounter weekend or some other marriage enrichment program, or spend a weekend away at a favorite, quiet place playing together with your spouse and children, discussing the goals of your marriage and family for the coming year.

Following these recommendations will help you assure the continued growth and health of your marriage.

Emergency Maintenance

Sometimes certain problems occur that require your taking your marriage into the shop. Yes, it can be expensive, and yes, it is always a pain, but keeping a marriage in good working order sometimes requires some professional assistance. How can you tell when its time for a check up?

Counseling is automatically indicated if...

• Your arguments are becoming physical.
• Many of your arguments occur while one or the other of you is drunk or high, or many of your arguments are over drinking or drug use.
• You are fantasizing about having an affair.
• You are spending more and more time with a friend of the opposite sex who you feel understands you better than your mate (even if your intentions are pure).
• You or your mate seem to be avoiding each other.
• When you look at your mate, you get a sinking feeling in your gut, or become angry and irritable for no reason.

Not every issue is cause for counseling, but some other issues (or combination of issues) may warrant special attention. Take the following quiz to see if you are due for a marital tune-up. Mark each statement "T" for true or "F" for false.

____My mate and I keep having the same arguments over and over.
____I often feel picked on by my mate.
____I often feel disappointed or let down by my mate.
____I wonder if my spouse really loves me.
____I feel that my mate is a controlling person.
____I think our arguments get out of control.
____I wonder if I married the right person.
____I intentionally avoid spending time with my mate.
____I feel like my mate doesn't understand me.
____I often think negatively about my mate.

0–1   No special maintenance required. Follow regular maintenance schedule as described above.
2–4   I recommend taking a marriage enrichment course, reading some books on marriage and family issues, and reviewing some of the exercises in *The Exceptional Seven Percent,* especially, Twenty-five Ways to Make Love—Every Day (page 90).
5+   I would recommend considering some counseling. Don't wait until the cancer is inoperable.

I would also like to offer my help with any technical assistance. I am available for telephone consultations, seminars, and other marriage and family enrichment experiences. Contact me at Professional Solutions, (740) 266-6461 or check out my website at www.exceptional marriages.com for more information.

May you live in health and happiness all the days of your life. And may the next Exceptional marriage I learn about be yours.

Bibliography

Allende, I. *Aphrodite: A Memoir of the Senses.* New York: HarperCollins, 1998.

Bandler, L. *Solutions.* San Rafael, CA: Future Pace, 1985.

Beck, A. *Love Is Never Enough.* New York: Houghton Mifflin, 1988.

Covey, S. *The Seven Habits of Highly Effective Families.* New York: Golden Books, 1997.

Diagnostic and Statistical Manual of Mental Disorders, 4th edition. Washington, DC: American Psychiatric Association, 1944.

Erikson, E. *Childhood and Society.* New York: W. W. Norton & Co., 1964.

Fowler, J. *Stages of Faith: The Psychology of Human Development and the Quest for Meaning.* San Francisco: Harper, 1995.

Gottman, J. *Why Marriages Succeed or Fail, And How You Can Make Yours Last.* New York: Simon & Schuster, 1994.

Hendrix, H. *Getting the Love You Want: A Guide for Couples.* New York: Harper Perennial, 1992.

Lederer, W. and Jackson, D. *The Mirages of Marriage.* New York: W. W. Norton and Co., 1968.

Lewis, C. S. *The Four Loves.* New York: Harcourt Brace, 1960.

Maslow, A. *Motivation and Personality, 2nd edition.* New York: Harper and Row, 1970.

Madanes, C. "Brief Therapy for Managed Care." Pittsburgh: Seminar—The Family Therapy Center of Maryland, Nov. 1997.

Moore, T. *The Soul of Sex: Cultivating Life as an Act of Love.* New York: HarperCollins, 1998.

Schnarch, D. *Passionate Marriage: Love, Sex, and Intimacy in Emotionally Committed Relationships.* New York: W. W. Norton and Co., 1997.

Schwartz, J. *Brain Lock: Free Yourself from Obsessive Compulsive Behavior.* New York: HarperCollins, 1997.

Schwartz, P. *Peer Marriage.* New York: Free Press, 1994.

Schwartz, R. *The 501 Best and Worst Things Ever Said About Marriage.* Secaucus, NJ: Citadel Press, 1995.

Smalley, G. *Hidden Keys of a Loving Lasting Marriage.* Grand Rapids, MI: Zondervan, 1988.

Sullivan, H.S. *Conceptions of Modern Psychiatry.* New York: W. W. Norton and Co., 1953.

Wallerstein, J. and Blakeslee, S. *The Good Marriage.* New York: Houghton Mifflin, 1995.

Index